GARRISON
LIFE AT
VINDOLANDA

A BAND OF
BROTHERS

Fratri karissimo

GARRISON
LIFE AT
VINDOLANDA

A BAND OF
BROTHERS

*Anthony
Birley*

TEMPUS

First published 2002

PUBLISHED IN THE UNITED KINGDOM BY:

Tempus Publishing Ltd
The Mill, Brimscombe Port
Stroud, Gloucestershire GL5 2QG
www.tempus-publishing.com

PUBLISHED IN THE UNITED STATES OF AMERICA BY:

Tempus Publishing Inc.
2 Cumberland Street
Charleston, SC 29401
1-888-313-2665
www.arcadiapublishing.com

Tempus books are available in France and Germany
from the following addresses:

Tempus Publishing Group   Tempus Publishing Group
21 Avenue de la République   Gustav-Adolf-Straße 3
37300 Joué-lès-Tours   99084 Erfurt
FRANCE   GERMANY

British Library Cataloguing in Publication Data.
A catalogue record for this book is available from the British Library.

ISBN 0 7524 1950 1

Typesetting and origination by Tempus Publishing.
PRINTED AND BOUND IN GREAT BRITAIN

Contents

List of illustrations

Text figures

Colour plates

Preface

We few, we happy few, we band of brothers

'If you love me, brother, send me some hunting-nets', begins a draft letter from the Vindolanda garrison commander, Flavius Cerialis, to his friend and colleague Brocchus. In their correspondence Cerialis and the other prefects known from the writing tablets regularly call one other 'brother', sometimes 'dearest brother'. For that matter, the soldiers also address their 'messmates' (*contibernales*) or 'fellow-soldiers' (*commilitones*) as 'brother'. The small number of women known clearly shared this sense of being part of a family – and not just the wives of officers, like Claudia Severa, wife of Brocchus, and her *soror karissima*, Cerialis' wife Sulpicia Lepidina; 'sister Thuttena' is greeted by Chrauttius in his letter to Veldedeius. Besides, there are signs that the garrison, Batavians and Tungrians, and their camp-followers, regarded themselves as superior to the natives, the *Brittunculi*. Hence the subtitle. I hope that the title *Garrison Life at Vindolanda* gives the right impression of the contents. I had been planning a book on these lines for over ten years. In *Vindolanda Research Reports* (*VRR*) II, I discussed the tablets period by period, from the first, *c.*AD 85-90, to the fifth, which began soon after 120, stressing names and origin of individuals. Space was limited: in the last note I commented that '[u]ltimately, a separate study of "The People of Vindolanda" may well be desirable'. That title was shortly afterwards more or less bespoken, when Alan Bowman, who, with David Thomas, has by now spent the best part of three decades deciphering the tablets, produced *Life and Letters on the Roman Frontier*, subtitled 'Vindolanda and its People'.

Peter Kemmis Betty and I first met in 1962, and worked together on *Life in Roman Britain*; and he published other books of mine in the 1970s and 1980s. I was delighted when he asked me to write this book in April 1999 and I suggested delivery in September 2001, confident that *TV* III, the edition by Alan Bowman and David Thomas of the many tablets found in 1991-4, would have appeared well before this. This has not happened after all. As in *VRR* II, I have had to do my best to read unpublished texts, mostly in discussion with Robin Birley; but helped in some cases by the editors' provisional readings, which they kindly made available. I have tried to cover the archaeological context, rather than just the content, of the tablets. Without liberal use of Robin's excavation report, *VRR* I, to an extent that would justify his suing me for plagiarism (but he tells me he does not object), this would have been impossible. I have also benefited from *VRR* III and IV and the reports on excavations from 1997 onwards.

In a few cases men already known to us emerged after 1900 years from the murky depths, 10 to 15 feet below the surface of a Northumberland field, contemporaries not just of emperors – Domitian, Nerva, Trajan, Hadrian – but of writers like Martial, Tacitus, the Younger Pliny, Juvenal and Suetonius. Some of our Vindolanda officers or their correspondents, for example Caecilius September, could easily have met Pliny, might even have known Tacitus. Several narrowly missed meeting Suetonius: he could easily have joined the 'band of brothers', but turned down the commission Pliny had secured him from Neratius Marcellus, 'my Consular', as Cerialis called his chief. As for emperors, there is strong evidence in one tablet that Hadrian, who arrived in Britain in AD 122 to launch his Wall project, was expected to stay at Vindolanda. Archaeological evidence suggests that suitable accommodation was prepared.

Many gaps remain in Romano-British history. The Vindolanda tablets have helped to fill a major one of these, the period between Agricola's retirement (AD 84) and the building of the Wall. Not least, we have several hundred names of people who lived in the frontier region – and even a few new place-names to try to identify. *To give to airy nothings* [or rather, mud-covered objects] *a local habitation and a name* (to adapt Shakespeare again) makes history and archaeology more exciting, at any rate more personal. Of course, interpretation does not stand still. I have sometimes misread unpublished tablets (mistakes are confessed here) or changed my mind about what they say or mean. In some important respects I take a different view to the editors, particularly on place-names in the addresses (ch. 1) and on expenditure and entertainment in Cerialis' household (ch. 7).

None of this work on Vindolanda would have been possible without Robin Birley's discoveries – not just of the tablets – and his continued recognition and recovery of more and more of these astonishing texts. His perseverance, versatility and sheer hard work in every conceivable way have built up Vindolanda into a great centre for visitors and a significant research institution. This book is not the place for autobiographical anecdotes (there are a few in ch. 1). Still, I am grateful that I have been able, almost every year that Robin has directed an excavation at Vindolanda (1967-76, 1981-5, 1991-5, and from 1997; not to mention 1949 and 1959), to participate for at least a few days, often a few weeks. This summer it was only two half-days, because I was finishing the book. Robin was still digging, deep down in the earliest levels again, as ever deploying not only camera and drawing board, but trowel, spade, shovel and wheelbarrow, with unequalled skill. I know better than most how much he has achieved, and am deeply grateful. Hence the dedication (cf. Martius to Victor, Inv. 1215).

A great many others, first and foremost Robin's wife Pat, have contributed to building up Vindolanda, and its Museum. The Trustees have played their part too, mostly behind the scenes. Several are no longer with us, including Daphne Archibald, who founded the Trust in 1970. All at Vindolanda greatly miss Eric Birley (1906-95), Chairman 1970-95, and Barri Jones (1936-99), Trustee for over 25 years. Many others deserve my thanks: at Vindolanda, Pat Birley, Andrew Birley, Barbara Birley, Justin Blake, Dryden Smith, Linda Thompson, Fiona Watson, as well as scores of volunteers who have wielded spades, picks, shovels and trowels, and pushed wheelbarrows with me over the past decades, especially my wife Heide; and for discussions and arguments about the tablets Jim Adams and Alan Bowman (long ago my colleagues at Manchester, both now at Oxford) and David Thomas. I have also benefited from the ideas and comments of my friends Paul Holder, Michael P. Speidel *patruus* and Michael A. Speidel *nepos*, and from Düsseldorf students who attended my classes (1990-1, 1993-4 and 2001) on the tablets. Düsseldorf's proximity to Batavian and Tungrian territory ought to have made me better informed than is actually the case about the archaeology of these countries. This makes me all the more grateful to Thomas Grünewald for inviting me to the Colloquia, at Xanten (1999) and Nijmegen (2001), which he organised with the late Jan-Kees Haalebos. Invitations to lecture on the tablets, in England and Wales, Germany, Italy, the Netherlands, Poland and the U.S.A. were gratefully accepted. Questions and discussion on these occasions were of great benefit to me, as was also the case after reports to Frontier Studies Congresses, at Carnuntum (1986), Canterbury (1989), Rolduc (1995) and Amman (2000).

David Woolliscroft supplied the air photographs and a fine view from the south. Most of the other illustrations were provided by Robin Birley and the Vindolanda team. Pictures of the tablets are all by Alison Rutherford, photographer *sans pareil*. The maps are my own work. For the rest of the book the usual disclaimer is required: much of what is any good is owed to others, errors are all mine.

If this book gives a little pleasure to those who know Vindolanda, I shall be content – and even more if it encourages any who have not yet been to come. To quote Flavius Cerialis (242): *cras bene mane Vindolandam veni*, 'tomorrow, early in the morning, come to Vindolanda'; or at least come as soon as possible. Site and museum are open most of the year, from 10a.m.

Note

References to the writing tablets are mostly given by a simple number in brackets: those published in *TV* II are numbered 118-573, unpublished ones have the Inventory numbering, 998-1617. They are generally cited without the prefix '*TV* II' or 'Inv.', except where there might be ambiguity, e.g. 'Inv.' is added for stylus tablets, all of which remain unpublished, and for one ink text omitted by *TV* II. In a few cases the 1983 publication is cited, as '*TV* I'.

1 Introduction

Vindolanda rediscovered: excavation old and new

The Romans were installed at Vindolanda by the later first century AD. They still had a garrison there, on paper at least, over 300 years later — its commander was one of the officers serving 'along the line of the Wall', *per lineam valli*, in the British section of the *Notitia Dignitatum*. Not long after 400, effective Roman control over Britain lapsed. A 'sub-Roman' population lingered on at Vindolanda, at least some of them Christians: a small chapel has been identified, built about 400, in the courtyard of the commander's residence, the *praetorium*. Another century or so later, a man called Brigomaglos was buried at Vindolanda, from his name a Briton of high rank, from the language of his epitaph a Christian. During the sixth century a small stone slate, with Christian symbols — a form of the *chi-rho* — was dropped in a house built over the silted-up south ditch. Before long new conquerors left a trace, a brooch found above the door-sill of the old south gate.[1]

1   The Christian chapel, c.AD 400

2   *The tombstone of Brigomaglos, c.AD 500*

3   *The chi-rho stone (11 x 8cm; 2cm thick)*

4   *The ninth-century strap-end*

These people, Angles, established a powerful kingdom, Bernicia, which, after union with its southern neighbour Deira, rose to still greater heights as Northumbria. Corbridge, next to Roman *Coria*, once so closely connected with Vindolanda, flourished then, as did a new foundation, 6km to its west, Hexham. But in these centuries Vindolanda seems to have been largely deserted, known at best locally perhaps as a source of building stone. The fort platform was ploughed. In the ninth century someone dropped a bronze strap-end there, in the twelfth a penny of Henry II was lost. Anglo-Scottish conflicts seriously affected travel and settlement. Wallace ravaged Northumberland and Cumberland in 1297. In 1306, Edward I, on his last campaign of many, stayed a night at Bradley Hall, less than a mile from Vindolanda. Peaceful visitors stayed away, it seems: the moss-troopers or Border Reivers saw to that. The first serious attempt to suppress them had to wait for the Union of the crowns, under James VI and I.

Antiquaries then began to take notice of Vindolanda. In 1702 the first account was published, by Christopher Hunter, who also registered, with a drawing, a newly unearthed inscription (*RIB* 1706). It recorded the restoration of a fort gate, with towers, in the early 220s. The text was then obliterated and the slab reworked for a gravestone in Beltingham churchyard, across the South Tyne. In about 1715, a little digging, probably in the *praetorium*, by John Warburton, an Excise officer, brought out a fine altar to 'the Fortune of the Roman People' (*RIB* 1684). It was saved, and is in Durham

5 *Plan of Vindolanda in the eighteenth century*

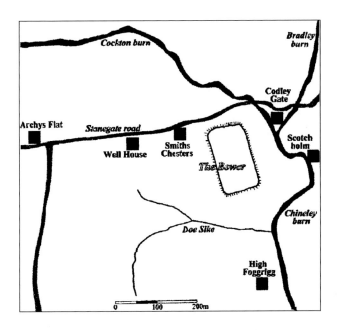

to this day. But more damage followed: as reported in 1769, masons looking for stone at the western end of the site removed what was thought to be a temple of Diana. The area was being resettled in the eighteenth century (the Act of Union in 1707 had finally brought security). New crofts were built, and the easily available materials were exploited. One small farm-house, Smith's Chesters, was built alongside the military bath-house west of the stone fort.

The first turning point came early in the nineteenth century. In 1814 the Rev. Anthony Hedley bought the small estate, Little Chesters as it was then known, which included, in the 'Camp Field', the site of fort and *vicus*. Four years on, a labourer, set to work by Hedley's tenant to dig up Roman stones for a field wall, uncovered a flight of steps leading to a gateway and to a 6ft high wall. He promptly destroyed the lot, but Hedley was able to save a fine tombstone (of Cornelius Victor, *RIB* 1713), although not the steps and walling. In January 1821 he gave a paper to the Society of Antiquaries of Newcastle upon Tyne, reporting what he had salvaged. Such wanton destruction was still the norm. Yet, as the foundation of the Antiquaries in 1813 demonstrated, informed interest was growing.

6   *The tombstone of Cornelius Victor (RIB 1713)*

'It is strange', Hedley told his audience, that despite extensive 'rifling' of all the Wall forts:

> nothing, or next to nothing, has been done towards systematically clearing the ground plan of one of these stations . . . Half a dozen labourers for a fortnight, at an expense of not more than five pounds, would clear away most of the rubbish from any one of these stations, and not only discover, it is to be hoped, many curious and precious fragments of antiquity, but throw a very interesting and desirable light on the stationary economy of the Romans, and on the form and arrangements of their *castra stativa*.

This highly optimistic proposal to 'clear' a Roman fort (using 'a portion of the funds of this Society') was not adopted. Instead, in 1829 Hedley began excavations at Vindolanda, systematic by the standards of the day, which continued until his death in January 1835. Meanwhile, in 1830-1, he had built himself a cottage, which he called Chesterholm, in a sheltered glade, across the Chineley burn below the fort's eastern rampart. Hedley was able to trace much of the defensive wall of the stone fort, to examine three of its four gates and to excavate part of the *praetorium*. In the centre of this building, in 1831, he found three large altars set up to the *Genius praetori* by commanders of the fourth Cohort of Gauls (*RIB* 1685-7).[2]

No further excavation took place for almost a century. Stone-robbing produced Brigomaglos' tombstone, recognised in 1878, and agricultural activity in 1914, near the western end of the 'Camp Field', turned up two altars, one fragmentary (*RIB* 1689), the other a splendid dedication (*RIB* 1700), by 'the villagers of Vindolanda', *vicani Vindolandesses*, to the god Vulcan, 'for the Divine House and for the Divinity of the Emperors'.[3] Eric Birley acquired Chesterholm and the adjacent farm, Codley Gate, in 1929. From 1930, when he was appointed Lecturer in Roman-British Archaeology at Armstrong College (now Newcastle University), until 1937, he explored parts of the site every year. Particularly important was the head-quarters building, *principia*; it was conserved after excavation. Under the civil settlement, *vicus*, west of the stone fort, he found late first-century occupation: timber buildings, ditches and a rampart. He inferred that there had been a timber Flavian fort, with long axis east and west, comparable in size and layout to the stone fort at Housesteads, and housing a milliary cohort.[4] Further research was prevented by the war; on its outbreak, he placed the stone fort in

7   *Hedley's cottage: Chesterholm*

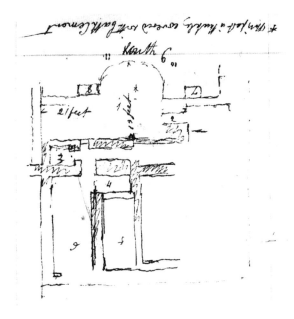

8   *Hedley's excavation of the praetorium (sketch by his friend John Hodgson)*

9   *Hedley's bookplate and signature (no portrait survives)*

10   *Codley Gate in 1935: the north-east corner of Vindolanda stone fort is at the top left*

11   Chesterholm in 1938

the Guardianship of the Office of Works (as the body was then called, the powers and duties of which have passed, after numerous other changes, to English Heritage). In 1950, too fully engaged as Master of Hatfield College, Durham to keep the place up, Eric Birley sold Chesterholm and Codley Gate farm (both then still lacking electricity, it must be added). Full-scale excavation did not begin again for over 20 years.

Robin Birley had two brief digs at Vindolanda, as a schoolboy in 1949 and as an undergraduate in 1956. In 1959 he excavated in the *vicus* for six weeks and from 1967–9 undertook a programme to explore it systematically. In the process, evidence for pre-Hadrianic occupation, including the line of a south rampart and ditches, was found in four places and Trajanic material and timber structures from the early forts (more than one, it was now clear) were sampled. But the main focus was on the civilian settlement of the later second and third centuries.[5] His results inspired a benefactress, Mrs Daphne Archibald, to purchase Codley Gate farm and with it the fort and *vicus*. A charitable Trust was formed in 1970, to which she presented the Camp Field. The Vindolanda Trust's Deed defines its aims as: the excavation of the Roman remains; their conservation for display to the public; the use of the site for training courses in archaeology; and the display of the finds in a good on-site museum. A new era had begun.

The excavation season of 1970 was, like those of previous years, relatively short, restricted to school holidays. But in April 1971 Robin Birley and his wife Pat gave up their teaching posts to work full time for the Trust, as they have done ever since.[6] Also in 1971, an unexpected opportunity was seized by the Trust: it was offered, and purchased, the small farm of Carvoran, seven miles west of Vindolanda. On this land

12 Eric Birley in his wartime role as an officer in MI

lies a Roman fort which, like Vindolanda, pre-dated Hadrian's Wall, and is on the same east-west Roman road, the Stanegate; but unlike Vindolanda, over 1km south of the Wall, Carvoran is at the point where Stanegate and the Wall converge. Yet for the time being no development could take place there.

In 1971-6, excavation at Vindolanda was able to carry on for at least half the year. The research aim was still to uncover and interpret as much as possible of the *vicus*. It all had to be done on a shoestring, with volunteer labour. But material support was provided by several local education authorities, which also paid fees for classes of older school students who attended training courses. And in due course visitors could be charged for entry to the site and (at first housed in a Nissen hut) museum. During work on the *vicus* – of which the stone buildings, including the military bath-house, were conserved – exploration of the Flavian and Trajanic forts that lay beneath it had been ruled out. But in 1972 new information about them suddenly emerged. There had been problems with flooding in several parts of the *vicus* excavation: both the natural drainage and the modern farm drains, flowing down into the Doe Sike south of the site, had been interrupted. To solve this problem, in late August, near the end of the excavating season, Robin Birley and half a dozen volunteers cut a long trench to lay a new 6in pipe, in a carefully selected area, not scheduled as an ancient monument, outside the south-west corner of the stone fort. They first had to go through hard iron slag from an adjacent Roman foundry, beneath which was brown clay. Then, less than 90cm below the surface, they found a mass of black, organic material; the trench began to fill with water. A pump was brought in, work was resumed – and in what had looked like subsoil firstly a piece of South Gaulish samian was found, then more pottery, leather, and three well-preserved pieces of textile. This clearly came from the early timber fort or forts. What Eric Birley had postulated in the 1930s was on the way to being documented in detail.

But it was in March 1973 that Robin Birley made his truly startling discovery: a writing tablet of a hitherto unknown type. The drainage trench which had yielded organic material the previous year was now carefully reopened and enlarged. Within a fortnight, in a 10ft (3m) square, bottomed at 13ft (3.9m), it revealed Roman posts still *in situ*. Further, there was a mass of leather, textiles, straw mixed with bracken, and wood of all kinds, from oak beams and planking to wattle-and-daub walling and twigs. Robin Birley then 'came across two small thin fragments of wood, which looked rather like oily plane shavings'. His assistant, invited to inspect one, 'passed it back, observing that it seemed to have some peculiar marks on it. I had another look and thought I must have been dreaming, for the marks appeared to be ink writing.' He summed up his reaction a few years later:

> If I have to spend the rest of my life working in dirty, wet trenches, I doubt whether I shall ever again experience the shock and excitement I felt at my first glimpse of ink hieroglyphics on tiny scraps of wood.[7]

These scraps, measuring together 16 x 3cm, proved to be part of a letter (*TV* I 38=II 346) to someone serving at Vindolanda *c.*AD 100. The unknown writer reported the dispatch 'from Sattua' of clothing and footwear, including underpants, *subligaria*, and socks, *udones*, and greeted some named 'messmates', *contibernales*. [8]

The two dozen or so words, some incomplete, could only be read by infra-red photography. It was to be some time before the appropriate conservation techniques were developed. Meanwhile, the right scholars were found to read Latin handwriting, David Thomas and Alan Bowman, from the Universities of Durham and Manchester respectively. Their first publications soon followed. Much publicity was generated and enormous interest shown, at home and abroad. A national Sunday newspaper sponsored six weeks of digging. Completely new methods had to be devised to excavate material of this kind. The earliest periods lay up to 4m below the modern surface, but the water-table was well above this. Water flowed in continuously at a depth of only 1.1m and thousands of gallons had to be pumped out of the trenches, from a sump. This had to be dug to prevent the Roman levels turning into a quagmire. Even so, it was often necessary to bucket out liquid mud. Another new factor was that successive Roman levels had been floored with a thick carpeting of bracken and straw – to counteract the damp – in which a great many of the writing tablets were embedded. To have trowelled the carpeting would have destroyed the tablets. Instead, it had to be cut out in blocks, like peat, and the bracken fronds carefully disengaged, peeled apart along the natural break lines.[9]

A helpful result of the publicity was the establishing of further contacts with specialists anxious to examine the environmental material – leather, textiles, wood,

13   *The first ink tablet found (TV II 346)*

14   *Excavation in the early levels: a pegged beam on the floor of a room in the Period III praetorium*

15   *Excavation in the early levels: wattle walls of Periods II-V crossing the line of the innermost Period I ditch; the base beam is of Period III*

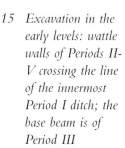

bones, bracken and the rest, and able to help with problems of conservation. Barri Jones, Professor at Manchester and a Trustee, had already introduced the Trust to Alan Bowman, and helped with initial conservation of the leather and timber. There was also, sadly, hostile criticism. Excavation methods used at Vindolanda were alleged to be (to paraphrase) cavalier and slipshod. This was a bit steep: it is doubtful whether any excavation in Britain, let alone one which had produced such important results, had ever taken place in such difficult conditions. Of course, digging, with the new methods described above, took place in front of visitors, who mostly had a close up view. A few complained. What they claimed or believed they had seen was not always what had actually been happening.[10]

The upshot was that the Dept of the Environment (DoE) appointed an 'Ad Hoc Committee' of eminent archaeologists, which, at the Trust's invitation, inspected the dig in summer 1974. Its report that autumn vindicated the Trust – but also insisted on various measures to improve the operation of what was recognised to be an exceptionally important excavation. Some were certainly sensible, others (in the Trust's view) impractical or unnecessary. Those that were practicable were implemented; for others (necessary or not) funds were simply not available. For example, one major item, undoubtedly desirable, was not then affordable: a fully equipped site laboratory in the museum, now in Chesterholm house, acquired that year (its purchase left the Trust with an overdraft that lasted for decades). This was given high priority, but could not be created at once. In the short term, the result was that after 1975, Robin Birley suspended excavation in the deep levels, from which the tablets and such a mass of organic material had come, for a decade. The Trust's budget could not finance excavation and post-excavation work on finds of this character as well as meeting its other commitments, let alone carrying out what had been called for by the Ad Hoc Committee. Excavation in 1976, lasting for over six months, concentrated on the *vicus*.

There was a great deal else to do. Robin was invited by Mortimer Wheeler to write a book about Vindolanda and his excavations, which was published in 1977. Work went on conserving and studying the finds, and a series of research reports was produced. The new museum had to be adapted and extended and the finds properly displayed; and its beautiful gardens were improved. The Trust's finances had to be put on a healthier basis, a continual uphill battle. In 1980 a new chance for research was offered: an excavation, funded jointly by the DoE and the Trust, was launched inside the stone fort, directed by Paul Bidwell. Several years' work were envisaged. In the event only one full season was possible: the Trust could not continue to fund its half of the costs. Fortunately, the DoE alone could finance post-excavation work for several years. By June 1983 Paul Bidwell's very substantial volume (with contributions by numerous specialists) was complete, and it was published in 1985. As well as a detailed report on his own excavations, he surveyed previous research and offered a reinterpretation of many aspects.

Meanwhile, there had been other important developments. In 1981 the British Museum agreed to purchase the writing tablets. Objects so tiny and delicate – as light as blotting paper after conservation – needed to be displayed in a controlled environment, with the right temperature and humidity. Further, security was vital – it was not so much that burglars might steal the tablets; but they might have been destroyed by fire or by vandalism. Also in 1981 the new Roman Army Museum was opened, at Carvoran. The Trust, unable to invest any funds there, had let the fields out as grass-parks; and in 1974, needing capital to purchase Chesterholm house, it had sold the farmhouse and steadings to Gateshead Metropolitan Borough Council, which planned to turn it into a field centre for its schools. That never materialised, municipal funds were cut and in 1980 Gateshead offered to sell the property back to the Trust. But the Trustees had to decline. Robin and Pat Birley stepped in, raised a hefty mortgage, renovated the farmhouse as their own home and turned the steadings into a museum. The RAM, it may be added, at once filled a gap for visitors to the Wall. In 1997 the Vindolanda Trust finally took over its administration.[11]

In spring 1983 came the complete publication of the writing tablets. Only three full texts, one letter and two documents, had been published in advance, in articles. It had been a long wait for the rest, ten years since the finding of the first examples, eight since the latest. As Alan Bowman and David Thomas explained, difficulties with conservation and photography, not solved until 1979, had delayed the research. They and all involved owe a particular debt to Alison Rutherford's photographic skills and patience (still at the service of the Trust nearly 30 years on). The volume (abbreviated here *TV* I) has a detailed introduction, including discussion of the tablets' format and nature, lettering forms and, based on the advice of Jim Adams, the Latin. The texts amount to 117 items: 11 documents, nos 1-11, and 23 letters, nos 21-6, 30-32, 34-5, 37-48, are discussed in detail, interspersed with another 14 texts, 'Descripta', assigned to one of these categories but too scrappy for more than brief presentation. Nos 49-88 are further 'Descripta', tablets on which at best only a few words, at worst just odd bits of lettering were legible; they are followed by 89-106, 'Texts of uncertain nature', of which nothing could be read, and 107-17, 'Stylus tablets', two with illegible ink writing, the rest with at best some incisions, all indecipherable (bar a single word).

The finding of the tablets had created a 'small sensation'; their full publication was greeted as exemplary.[12] This was new information on the 'stationary economy' of the Romans of a kind that Hedley could hardly have hoped for in his dreams. Further, the tablets shed new light on army organisation, the Latin language, Roman handwriting and above all on writing materials and literacy. For the history of Britain and the 'microhistory' of Vindolanda and the northern frontier zone there was some welcome precision, of the sort excavators relying on pottery, coins and occasionally a stone inscription could hardly expect. One tablet (*TV* I 37=II 225) supplied a documentary date for one level: it named the governor of Britain Neratius Marcellus, known to have been in office on 19 January 103. Others showed that the regiments in garrison included the First Tungrians and the Batavians (their number was still read in 1983 as the 'Eighth', otherwise unknown: it was really the Ninth, cf. below), of which the prefect was a man called Flavius Cerialis, recorded on at least two, perhaps on five tablets.

16 *Part of tablet 225. The governor Marcellus' name is in the top line; his title can be seen below*

That the tablets were now in the public domain was a great incentive to the Trust to resume excavation in the deep levels. Chesterholm House was now well equipped as a museum and research centre; enthusiasm among Robin Birley's team was high. Permission was granted by the DoE and a research programme began in spring 1985; it continued until June 1989. Results exceeded all expectations: the inventory numbering for writing tablets reached 339 in the first year, 610 by the end of 1986, 810 in 1987 and 970 in 1988. In 1989, a short half season, a mere 27, over half of them stylus tablets, were added. The grand total was thus just under 1000. To be sure, some proved after conservation not to be writing tablets or to be blank (as indeed had been the case with some found in 1973-5); or were stylus tablets (125 all told, then as now mostly indecipherable). Yet sometimes a single inventory number proved to cover more than one tablet.[13]

It would be quite wrong to give the impression that the writing tablets were the only significant finds. The damp but anaerobic conditions which preserved them also ensured the survival of textiles, wood, leather, leaves, bracken, even pupae of stable flies and a whole lot more. Metal was preserved in unusually good condition, with bronze coins and other objects coming out looking like gold. A clearer chronology of the timber forts was now possible, with more detail on their internal buildings and layout (naturally supplemented and refined by further digging from 1991-4). Remains of other Roman timber forts can be examined by finding post-holes and foundation-trenches. At Vindolanda – admittedly in often appalling conditions, in deep and watery trenches, often made intolerable by fumes or marsh-gas – the posts themselves, the beams and the internal wattle and daub walling can still be seen.

All the same, once again the tablets were the real treasure trove. There were not only far more than in the 1970s. Their content was more informative, indeed more exciting. A few highlights may be mentioned (in order of discovery). The 1985 season produced a memorandum on the *Brittones'* poor skills with weapons,

17 *The Batavians at Vindolanda were the Ninth Cohort (coh. VIIII: 175)*

18 *Flavius Cerialis: the man most often named in the tablets. This was the beginning of a draft letter (237) that was never written*

also calling them *Brittunculi* (a new, not very friendly word) (164); a birthday invitation from Cl(audia) Severa to Sulpicia Lepidina, wife of Flavius Cerialis (291); a line from Virgil's *Aeneid* (118), written in rustic capitals on the back of a draft letter (331), and more examples of a series of texts, not previously identified – all being very fragmentary (e.g. *TV* I 2, 12, 47, cf. II 151, 127, 152) – but now seen to be formulaic military reports, or *renuntia*. In 1986 came a letter from the delightfully named Chrauttius to his old messmate Veldedeius, the governor's groom (310); the 1987 season produced an account, including large amounts of beer, datable by the consuls of AD 111 (186); 1988 a strength report of the First Tungrians from the period I ditch (154), a corn distribution list (180) with a draft letter of protest about a beating on the back (344) and a very long letter, 46 lines, from a man called Octavius (343). Five shorthand texts were also found (122-6: still undeciphered), and more and more items concerning the prefect Flavius Cerialis and his wife Sulpicia Lepidina (already there but not recognised in *TV* I 25; cf. II 247). Cerialis' regiment was now clearly identified as the Ninth Batavians, not the Eighth (to be relegated to the category of 'phantom' units): the numeral was regularly written as VIIII rather than IX. To complicate the issue, the Ninth's sister regiment, the Third Batavians, was also in the vicinity: a letter to a man in the Third was found at Vindolanda (311), showing that a previously published letter (*TV* I 23) where *coh. VIII* had been read, also referred to *coh. III* (263). New finds also showed that a prefect of the First Tungrians thought to have been called Crispinus (*TV* I 30-33) was really called Priscinus (*TV* II 173, 295-8, perhaps 448). In many specimens of Roman handwriting, C and P are virtually identical.

A few of the new tablets were published fairly rapidly after their discovery, as the Trust had hoped and urged. The rest did not get into print until 1994: in *TV* II, a handsome volume, again edited by Bowman and Thomas, published by the British Museum. It included improved readings of many of the texts from the 1983 monograph, which can now be labelled *TV* I. The numbering runs from 118, following on from that of *TV* I, up to 573. Many but nowhere near all the texts are illustrated. There are 32 plates, with a total of 77 photographs, taken by D. Webb of the British Museum photographic service. They are of high quality, if not obviously superior to the 'excellent infra-red photographs taken by Alison Rutherford', without which, as the editors write in their preface, 'it would not have been possible to read these texts at all'. The Trust's 'Scheduled Monument Consent' (SMC) from English Heritage had ended with the short 1989 season. Permission for renewed excavation was dependent, as the (very desirable) regulations now lay down, on completing a report on what had been already dug. Robin Birley had lost no time in beginning this task; English Heritage itself agreed to publish the report when it was ready, and offered the services of its drawing office in London for the small finds illustrations. Contributions were obtained from those specialists who could be persuaded to produce interim discussions.[14]

The main report was delivered to the Heritage editor by the end of 1990. This fulfilled the necessary conditions and a new SMC was issued. From 1991 to 1994

more and more detail came to light about the early forts – and many more tablets
or potential tablets were inventoried, conserved and, if written on, photographed
by Alison Rutherford. In each of the first two years, inventory numbers only
climbed by a hundred or so, from 998 to 1104 and 1105 to 1206; but in 1993 they
leapt from 1207 to 1566; 1994, when the dig reached an area heavily disturbed by
the later stone fort, produced only a modest crop that brought the total to 1617.
The excavation report clearly needed to be updated. But, with no publication by
Heritage being imminent, the Trust decided to do it 'in house', in three instal-
ments of the *Vindolanda Research Reports*, new series, *VRR*. Two supporting
volumes on major finds, II and III, appeared first, in 1993, I, the excavation report
proper, in 1994.

As for the newly found tablets, the Trust was at first unwilling to ask the same
editors to deal with them, for fear that it would cause those from 1985-7 to appear
even later. In any case, only four tablets from 1991-2 had seemed substantial and
interesting. They were published by members of the Trust in 1994.[15] The intention
was to do likewise with further finds. As it turned out, the harvest in 1993 was so
great, and some items so interesting, that this policy was reversed. Shortly after *TV*
II appeared, Alan Bowman and David Thomas were handed photographs of the
tablets from 1991-3 (and in due course of the few from 1994). They produced a
preliminary edition of three especially interesting ones – the *expensa* of Flavius
Cerialis (1474A), the long and detailed invoice, with prices, of goods delivered
(1398) and the letter to Cerialis by the decurion Masclus, asking for more beer to
be sent (1544) – in autumn 1996. They estimated that of those found in 1991-3,
'there are between 70 and 80 substantial new ink texts which we hope to publish
within the next three years.'[16] Three years have stretched to five, as happens, and
TV III is still awaited.

Before 1983, no one involved in the excavations had felt remotely capable of
reading these texts themselves. After *TV* I appeared, Robin and I had no hesitation: we must learn to read Roman cursive ourselves. This would no doubt have
been an impossible aim without the help of the introduction to *TV* I (not least the
analysis of the letter-forms) and of course of the texts themselves in conjunction
with photographs. Robin could now tell straightaway in many cases, in the trench,
if the tablet was a letter or another sort of document; often a great deal more. An
infra-red document viewer, of the kind used by the police, soon gave him further
insight – he could find out in advance of conservation which tablets were blank
and which had writing on them (much of which he often read at this stage). The
new tablets were put now put into treatment in the Vindolanda within a few hours
of being found. After conservation, they were (in favourable cases) legible at least
in part. But almost all were easier to decipher in Alison Rutherford's photographs
than in the original.

Those who had been involved with Vindolanda for so long had a compelling urge
to try to decipher these messages from the past – and, it must be added, in case of
success to shout the results from the rooftops. This was evidently at odds with papy-
rological convention. Practitioners of that science are reluctant to make readings

public until they are completely confident they are right. Yet the tablets are not papyri; to those who have found them and have to report on the excavations, they are vitally important finds, the content of which, in most cases, once read, the archaeological team is very well qualified to interpret. Long waiting for information can be profoundly irritating. There has been no alternative to 'do it yourself'. The editors of *TV* I and II may have been amused, at best, from time to time annoyed, by what seemed premature and inaccurate attempts by unqualified persons. Apart from publishing the four tablets from the early 1990s, we have over the past 15 years quoted in print from a good many other unpublished texts; and published photographs of them.[17] Sometimes mistaken readings have been produced – but then not a few in *TV* I proved to be wrong (and corrections are already needed to *TV* II). That is the nature of the material.

In the Trust's view publication of all the texts should be rapid, and all with photographs. A complete edition can follow later. Further, the Trust believes that the archaeological context of each tablet deserves careful consideration. It is a pity to dispense with this, on the grounds that 'there are, understandably, a significant number of tablets in which the content does not fit the archaeological context to which they are assigned, and it is a well-known fact of archaeological life that objects are not infrequently found in strata where they do not belong.'[18] *TV* II, it was unfortunate, appeared at the same time as *VRR* I, the detailed excavation report. Study of this would have been much more useful than study of 'A review of the tablets, by periods', in *VRR* II, which came out a year earlier and to which the editors of *TV* II could and did refer (and repeatedly corrected). That contribution to *VRR* II had been written without access to more than a handful of provisional readings of texts that were to appear in *TV* II, and, for that matter, without access to *VRR* I.[19]

After a pause of two years, excavation resumed in 1997, with the help of a new generation of trained archaeologists, who had started digging at Vindolanda in their schooldays and had then studied the subject at university. From then until 2000, attention was focused on the stone fort. The results, all published year by year, predominantly relate to the third and fourth centuries and beyond. Something will be said about these aspects in the last chapter of this book. There were some exceptions, a few discoveries throwing light on the period of the tablets. In 1997, part of a tombstone was found, commemorating a centurion of the Tungrians (clearly the First), perhaps their acting commander, who had been 'killed in the war'. It had been reused as a building block in a late fourth-century structure in the *praetorium*. There are good reasons to associate this with the British rebellion at the start of Hadrian's reign.[20] The *praetorium* excavation also found traces here and there of the timber forts, or of their effects on the foundations of the stone periods above them.[21] In 1999 and 2000 further traces of the early forts were found, including part of the ditch of the Period I timber fort, outside the south wall of the stone fort; and within the fort, in the south-west corner, structures from Periods III, IV or V were discovered, much disturbed by later Roman building. Most exciting of all, the military bath-house, which must be the one mentioned in a Period III writing-tablet (155) as under construction, was located outside the south-east angle of the early fort, and fully excavated.[22]

In 2001 excavation in the deep levels was renewed, well to the west of the previously explored area. First results are extremely promising. Not least, it turns out that the Period I fort had multiple ditches on the west side. A separate discovery, at the westernmost end of the site, close to the Stanegate, was a temple of typical Celtic-Roman design, probably from the early second century and hence perhaps the *fanum* guarded by Amabilis (180, line 10). In front of the entrance a small altar was recovered, dedicated to a god who might be the Batavians' chief deity, Magusanus. In the meantime other publications have been appearing: *VRR IV, The Small Finds*, is appearing in fascicules. So far these have covered *The Weapons* (1996); *Security: the Keys and Locks* (1997), *The Tools* and *The Writing Materials* (both 1999). This last is a topic to which the rest of this introduction is devoted.

Writing tablets

Apart from papyrus, principally grown in Egypt and exported all over the Mediterranean, or the even more expensive parchment, there were alternative writing materials in the ancient world, including tablets made of wood. These are known to have been in general use. Thousands of examples have been found all over the Roman Empire, including over 250 at Vindolanda. They were made of spruce or larch, and hence must have been imported to Britain. The front of the tablet was hollowed out and filled with beeswax, the back generally left smooth. They vary in size, but the majority found at Vindolanda measure about 15 x 10cm and 0.5cm thick at the rim.[23] The wax surface was incised with a stylus,[24] a metal pen tapering to a point at one end, flattened into an eraser at the other. This surface could be smoothed or renewed when the text was no longer required, and the tablet reused. In virtually all cases the wax has perished. On one specimen from Vindolanda (Inv. 836) it survived: the lettering traces showed up white against the black stain of the wax, but after conservation most of the stain was lost. Often traces of the script went through the wax onto the wood and this lettering can sometimes be read. But the task of distinguishing between multiple superimposed scripts is generally hopeless. It is easier to read the addresses on the back, especially those written in larger lettering. So far, however, most of the stylus tablets, which up till 1994 made up a little under 20% of all the writing tablets, remain undeciphered.[25]

What has made Vindolanda so special is the discovery of the 'leaf' tablets, written on with ink. These were scarcely known before the Vindolanda finds of 1973: subsequently other sites, notably Luguvalium (Carlisle), have yielded specimens.[26] Some of the best preserved Vindolanda examples, such as the birthday invitation to Lepidina (291), Chrauttius' letter to Veldedeius (310), the decurion Masclus' request to send more beer for the comrades (1544), the draft letter of protest – intended (I believe) to be handed to the Emperor Hadrian – by a man who had been beaten (344) and Octavius' letter about his financial crisis

19 Inv. 836: a stylus tablet before conservation

20 Inv. 836: after conservation

(343), are particularly exciting. But even short fragments of letters are like voices from the distant past, giving direct insight into the lives of the men and women who first wrote and read these letters 1900 years ago. Several of the documents are also very illuminating, especially the report on the *Brittunculi* (160) and the *expensa* from the *praetorium* of Cerialis (1474A).

Whereas 'waxed tablets', *tabellae ceratae* (and letter-carriers, *tabellarii*), nicknamed *pugillares*, literally 'fistfuls', are mentioned often enough in classical literature, leaf tablets at first sight seldom crop up. Their widespread use was probably an innovation in the north-west of the empire, where papyrus was too expensive for everyday use. They could be called *pugillares*, it seems, but may have had another name, or

21   An address on a stylus tablet: Inv. 805, with the name SEQVENTINIVM

nickname, as well. Pliny the Elder, who had quite likely come across them as an officer in Rhineland in the late 50s, may have called them *sectiles*, '(thin) slices', or *laminae*, 'sheets' (as in a sheet of metal or paper), made, in this case, from maple wood. This prolific author no doubt much appreciated such cheap substitutes for papyrus – which were certainly also much cheaper than the standard wax tablets. He apparently used them for making the tens of thousands of notes on which his vast *Natural History* was based.[27]

Complete leaf tablets are generally some 20 x 9cm, the thickness varying between 0.25 and 3mm. They were normally scored down the centre, to allow them to be folded. Some also had tie-holes and two V-notches, so that they could be tied with thread and sealed; and it was possible to tie several such leaves together to form a 'concertina' like document or small notebook. The surface was carefully smoothed and obviously treated in some way, by sizing, to ensure that the ink would not run. Most tablets were made of alder, a few of birch and one or two apparently of oak. For some reason those used for letters were written along the grain of the wood, accounts, invoices, lists and the like across the grain. The space available was relatively restricted compared with the stylus tablet, in most cases not much more than eight or nine lines for each leaf. The ink was made of carbon and gum arabic.

Punctuation of the modern kind was not used, except in some cases when a stop was written between words (although not between prepositions and the nouns following them). The apex, like an acute accent, was also used, in most cases correctly – to indicate a long vowel – although sometimes short vowels were given one. The few still indecipherable shorthand texts have already been mentioned. There are also a few drawings or doodles. The ink tablets, it is clear, were ephemera, not designed to be kept for long. For longer term records, legal contracts and financial transactions, the more solid and expensive stylus tablets were available. They could be kept in boxes, like fat filing cards, with the advantage that – as examples from Vindolanda now reveal – the subject could be written in ink on the rim, for ready retrieval. Stylus tablets were, of course, still regularly used for letters as well.

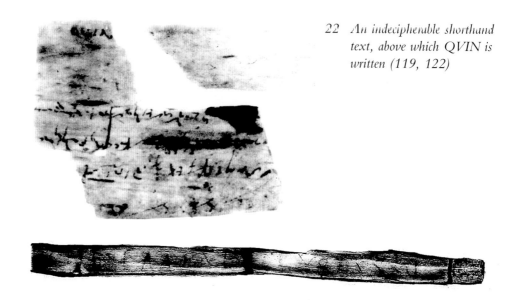

22 *An indecipherable shorthand
    text, above which QVIN is
    written (119, 122)*

23 *An ink inscription on the rim of a stylus tablet: Inv. 561/2*

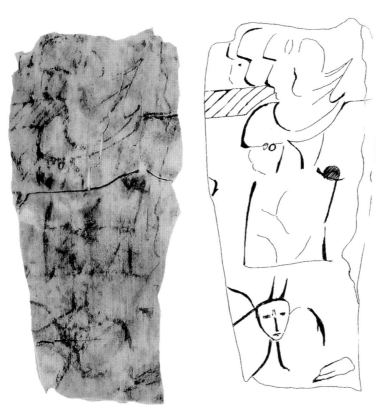

24 *A drawing:
    Inv. 616*

Pens

Over 200 styli have been found, with as many as nine different types, made of good quality iron, some being decorated with bronze leaf. The basic pen was probably produced by a black-smith, then a specialist craftsman, using a lathe, added the sometimes elaborate chevron patterns and other refinements, including the bronze leaf or inlay. Given the much higher number of leaf-tablets, written on with ink, than stylus tablets, it is puzzling that the statistics for pens are diametrically opposite. Of over 200 styli, only nine are of the iron nib type with a wooden holder designed to write with ink. It may be, of course, that reed or quill pens were mainly used for writing with ink, but none have so far been identified, though they would have been well preserved, like the other organic materials. The iron nib ink pens are not unique to Vindolanda: they have been found often enough in Britain and elsewhere, but are described as ox-goads. They could perhaps have been used for this purpose; however, the Vindolanda examples really were used as pens. One still bore traces of ink at the foot of the shaft, and experimentation with two others showed that three or four words could be written with a single dip into a modern ink. Further, the wooden shank, in three cases preserved in whole or part and still attached to the nib, had a narrow hole bored down the centre, making it in effect a fountain pen.[28]

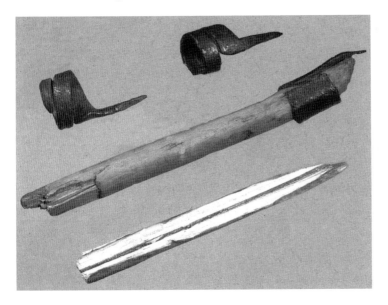

26   Ink pens with iron nib and wooden shank

25   A stylus for writing on wax

Addresses

The question how letters from and to Vindolanda were delivered is to some extent answered by the texts themselves. Flavius Cerialis begins his draft letter to Crispinus (225) with the words: 'as Grattius Crispinus is returning . . . I have gladly embraced the opportunity of greeting you'. Clearly, Grattius was going to take Cerialis' letter with him. Two other letters begin with very similar expressions: 'I have embraced the opportunity of writing' (212), 'I have not let pass, Lord, the opportunity when it was first offered . . . ' (1254). Officers also used soldiers as couriers. Priscinus sent two men from the First Cohort of Tungrians all the way to Bremetennacum (Ribchester) with a letter for the governor – who had gone by the time they arrived; Priscinus' colleague at Bremetennacum sent them on, he reported to Priscinus, perhaps to Lindum (Lincoln), if the name has been read correctly (295). Two letters to Cerialis have the same phrase, 'I have sent you . . . through a cavalryman' (252, 268); a third (318), probably also to him, has a slightly more elaborate expression, 'I have sent you, from the cohort of which I am in command'. The decurion Vitalis (263) actually names the bearer of his previous letter to Cerialis, sent on 30 April, 'which you received from Equester, centurion of the Third Cohort of Batavians'. A fragment from period IV (1103) reads: 'the letter which [I sent?] you through Su[. . .]'. Major, writing to Cocceius Maritimus (1022A), adds a postscript: 'If you are going to send a boy (i.e. a slave), send a note of hand with him, so that I may be safer.' Martius writes to his friend Victor (1215): 'I ask that you write to me through an *optio*'. This surely meant: 'write to me and get an *optio* (an NCO) to bring the letter'.

In other words, people waited until they heard someone was travelling to or past the place to which they wanted to write. Otherwise, if the business was urgent (and official), an officer could send one or more soldiers with a letter. Or, as Major expected Maritimus to do, one could get a slave to act as courier. At the topmost end of the Roman hierarchy, the governor had men whose regular duties included delivery of his letters. Veldedeius, *equisio cos.*, 'the Consular's groom' (310), is probably an example. In the letter sent to him, it may be noted, his correspondent Chrauttius took the chance of telling Veldedeius to ask the vet Virilis 'whether you may send through someone from our people the shears which he promised me at a price'. 'Someone from our people', *aliquem de nostris*, immediately intelligible to Veldedeius, is less clear to us – does it mean 'one of the Batavians'? At all events, it meant that someone due to travel from Vindolanda to London would be asked to take the shears with him for Chrauttius – or would the journey have been the other way round, from London to Vindolanda, or to wherever else Chrauttius was based?

This is a problem of interpretation. A limited number of the letters preserve an address on the back. In the fullest form it is composed as follows: at the top (sometimes in the left-hand corner) there is a place-name, in the locative case (or its equivalent, so it seems); then comes, often in elongated script, the name of the recipient of the letter, in the dative, sometimes followed by his rank; finally, at the

27   The address on TV II 310

bottom left (sometimes slanting diagonally upwards) comes the name of the writer, in smaller lettering, preceded by *a* or *ab*, 'from', sometimes followed by his rank or some other identification. On the back of Chrauttius' letter, the address is laid out as follows:

Londini	at London
Veldedeio	to Veldedeius
equisioni cos	Consular's groom
a Chrauttio	from Chrauttius
fratre	(his) brother

It is argued that 'at London' should be understood with 'to Veldedeius', and, of course, the governor's groom would normally be based at London (by now the provincial capital), if not invariably: when the governor travelled, his groom would go too. As to why the letter was found at Vindolanda, rather than at London, the answer could be simply that Veldedeius brought it with him, when at Vindolanda on the governor's business. His presence in the *praetorium* of Flavius Cerialis is indeed attested independently, by a leather offcut bearing his name.

All the same, a difficulty is that of those letters which preserve a full address, with place-name, the majority name somewhere other than Vindolanda. As well as *Londini*, *Coris*, 'at Coria' (Corbridge), occurs three times (312, Inv. 722, 1215); *Eburaci/o*, 'at Eburacum' (York), twice (Inv. 575, 1220); *Catarac(tonio)*, 'at Cataractonium' (Catterick), twice (Inv. 836, 1145, the latter abbreviated), and *Vinovis*, 'at Vinovia' (Binchester) once (Inv. 851). Some other cases are not clear, either because the lettering is hardly legible or because it is uncertain whether it was part of an address (Inv. 1110, 1135III, 1359). On a letter to Flavius Cerialis (271), the incompletely preserved place-name begins *Vi* . . . , yet the editors concede that 'it is very hard to read what follows as part of *Vindolandae*'.[29] All the same, there are six addresses with *Vindolandae* or an abbreviated form of the name (338, 343, Inv. 689, 1022, 1520A, 1581). But apart from one (343), which only has *Vindol*, and nothing else – no names of recipient or writer – the others might be drafts written at Vindolanda. Major's letter, for example, was written in bed, or as he himself put it, while 'I am making the bed warm'. It is splattered with ink blotches in places, a good reason for this tablet to have been retained and a fair copy sent.

In fact, given that letters were entrusted to couriers known to the writer, there was no point in adding the address of the recipient. There may be one exception, a letter from Sollemnis to Paris (311). In this case the addressee's name in the dative is followed by what could be read as 'at Ulucium in the fort of the Third Cohort of Batavians', *Paridi Ulucio cas[tris coh]ortis III Batavorum*. (Ulucium was probably not far away from Vindolanda, cf. below chapter 2.) As for the letter (343) which only has *Vindol* on the back, and not even the name of the recipient, Candidus, it is surely conceivable that the writer, Octavius, actually wrote the letter *at* Vindolanda and left it there to be collected, because Candidus, with whom he clearly had urgent business to transact, was not there when he called. There are other possible explanations as well.[30]

28   The address on TV II 311

An address on the back of a stylus tablet found at Carlisle (*RIB* II 2443.10) is thought to decide the question. It reads *Trimontio aut Lugu(v)a[l]io M. Iulio Martiali*, 'at Trimontium (Newstead) or Luguvalium to Marcus Julius Martialis'. It is argued that '[t]his is a conclusive piece of evidence since it clearly cannot refer to the place of writing and *must* refer to the places *to* one of which the letter was to be delivered (i.e. the sender was uncertain whether the addressee was at Trimontium or Luguvalium)'. Yet the writer may not have been sure, when he wrote the address, whether he was still going to be at Trimontium or would already have moved on to Luguvalium by the time he could find someone to take the letter to its recipient.[31] In any case, the letter to Julius Martialis lacks both the recipient's rank and the writer's name; hence it is not an exact parallel to the Chrauttius' letter to Veldedeius. A 'further, decisive, piece of evidence' has been adduced, an instruction in a papyrus letter from a sailor: *et si scr[i]bes mihi epistulam inscribas in liburna N[e]ptuni*, 'If you write me a letter, address it "On the ship Neptune".'[32] This, however, could be just another way of addressing the letter, similar to the Vindolanda example already cited: 'to Paris at Ulucium in the fort of the Third Cohort of Batavians'.

A completely preserved letter headed on the back 'at Vindolanda' written to someone known to have been there, such as Flavius Cerialis, would prove the case for the place-name being the destination – or a letter written to Cerialis headed, for example, 'at London' would surely indicate that it was the place from which the letter was written.[33] Meanwhile, other comparisons can be made. Most letters by or to Cicero do not give a place of writing – or, for that matter, a destination. The details may have been deleted by early editors. But there are some exceptions: for example, letters he wrote from exile (58-57 BC) have at the end *data*, 'dispatched', the date and a locative place-name, e.g. 'at Thessalonica' (*Ad Att.* 3.8ff.). Some of his correspondents' letters likewise end with a date and a locative, for example 'at Perge' (*Ad fam.* 12.14-15).[34] In these cases the place was obviously the place of writing or from which the letter was dispatched. A much later example, the letter quoted on a famous monument in Normandy, the 'Marbre de Thorigny', was written by a governor of Lower Britain *c.*AD 220, Tiberius Claudius Paulinus, to his Gallic protégé, Titus Sennius Sollemnis. No place of destination is named, but the place where the letter was sent from is given, *a Tampio*, 'from Tampium'.[35] Likewise, a patron of Caere in Etruria, writing to the magistrates and councillors of that town, ends his letter *data prid. Idus Septembr. Ameriae*, 'dispatched on 12 September at Ameria'.[36] Many letters from emperors, recorded on stone, register, at the end, where the letter was sent from or where it was written: thus *in Albano*, 'in the Alban residence'. A convenient collection includes imperial letters 'dispatched' from Neapolis, Antium, Dyrrhachium, Juliopolis, Laodicea-on-Lycus; at Athens; [from or in the villa] Tiburtina; from Rome; at Rome; from Viminacium, Capua; at Rome; from Antioch.[37]

As for the invoices listing goods delivered to Vindolanda, the supplier will in many, perhaps in most cases, have delivered the goods, with delivery note, himself. In one case a letter (309) reveals that a haulier was used: 'Metto to his Advectus very

29   *Metto's delivery note in the form of a letter (309)*

30   *Goods ordered from London through Adiutor (Inv. 1503B)*

many greetings. I have sent you timber through Saco' – there follows a list, taking up the next 11 lines, of the items sent, very much in the form of a straightforward delivery note; but all the same Metto ends up with good wishes: 'I pray that you have good health, brother'. Another tablet (1503B) opens with the words 'Dispatched from Londinium through Adiutor', the latter either the carrier or perhaps the slave or soldier sent from Vindolanda to obtain the goods.

2 Batavians and Tungrians

The battle [of Mons Graupius] opened with fighting at long range: the Britons not only stood firm but displayed skill in parrying the javelins of our men . . . while hurling a great rain of spears themselves. Then Agricola exhorted the four Batavian and two Tungrian cohorts to fight hand-to-hand at sword's point. This was what they had been trained for in their long service.

Tacitus, *Agricola* 36.1

One each of the Batavian and Tungrian cohorts singled out by Tacitus for their contribution to Agricola's great victory of AD 83 was stationed at Vindolanda in the Flavian and Trajanic periods. The First Cohort of Tungrians arrived two years or so after Mons

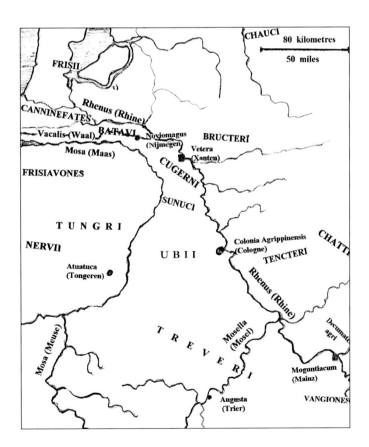

31 Map 1: Batavians and Tungrians and some of their neighbours

Graupius, but did not stay long, being replaced after five years or a little more by the Ninth Cohort of Batavians. The Batavians remained until 105. When they were withdrawn for service far afield, never to return to Britain, the First Tungrians returned to Vindolanda, this time for several decades. Compared to other units of the *auxilia*, the regiments formed from these two peoples were a little out of the ordinary: they continued to draw recruits from the country where they had been formed and were still commanded by members of their own aristocracy.

The Batavians

Writing in AD 98 (when the Ninth Batavians were at Vindolanda), Tacitus thus describes the Batavians:

> Of all these [German] states the outstanding in courage are the Batavi; they do not occupy much of the river-bank, but have the Rhine island. They were once a sept of the Chatti, but after an internal conflict migrated to their present territory, there to become part of the Roman Empire. Their honourable status and the distinction of the old alliance still remain: they are not humiliated by tribute, nor does the tax-farmer grind them down. Exempt from burdens and special contributions and set aside exclusively for use in battle, they are reserved, like spears and other weapons, for war. (*Germany* 29.1)

He repeats this account in the *Histories* (4.12), written a few years later, with an additional comment: the Batavians' new home in the Lower Rhineland had been uninhabited when they arrived there. They may have claimed this. Archaeology shows that it was not the case; however, the immigrants clearly became the new elite among the existing – Gallic or Celtic – population.[1]

Tacitus does not say when they migrated from Chattan territory – in the northern part of modern Hesse in central Germany – to the 'Rhine island', between the old Rhine and the Waal. Their chief place there was called first Batavodurum, 'Fort of the Batavians', later, when rebuilt after the revolt of AD 70, Noviomagus, 'New Market'. Both names are Celtic. Noviomagus lies beneath modern Nijmegen in the Netherlands – near which the district 'Betuwe' still recalls the ancient inhabitants. A passage in Caesar's *Gallic War* (4.10) suggests that the Batavians had already arrived in his day, at latest in the 50s BC: 'The Meuse (*Mosa*) flows from the Vosges mountains . . . and receiving from the Rhine a tributary called the Waal (*Vacalus*) forms the island of the Batavi'. The passage is generally regarded as a later interpolation and most believe that they split off from the Chatti some time after Caesar's campaigns.

Whenever it occurred, their name alone provides a nice clue to the background of this move: *batavi* means 'the better ones' – surely a self-description.[2] One may infer that they had been an elite – perhaps pro-Roman – group among the Chatti, deposed after a power struggle. Tacitus' information seems to be confirmed by coin evidence. Gold coins, found mainly in Chattan territory, on which a *triquetrum*, or trefoil, is depicted, are closely matched by a mass of examples from the Batavian heartland, datable to the early Roman period. These evidently Batavian coins were at first of silver, later of billon, and unlike their Chattan prototypes, carried extra marks on the reverse, of which no fewer than 18 variants have been identified. These were perhaps the personal identifying symbols of successive Batavian leaders.[3]

By 52 BC Caesar had recruited German cavalry and some served with him in the Civil War that began in 49 BC, as far afield as Egypt, where they even rode into the Nile. It has been suggested that these men were principally Batavians, later renowned for their capacity to swim rivers in full battle gear. At all events, Batavians would soon provide the main contribution to a new elite unit, which served the Julio-Claudian emperors from Augustus to Nero as mounted bodyguards, stationed in Rome, the *Germani corpore custodes*. This unit was often called 'the Batavians'.[4] Augustus also formed a Batavian cavalry regiment, *ala Batavorum*. Commanded by a Batavian nobleman, Chariovalda, it fought for Rome in Germanicus' campaigns east of the Rhine (Tacitus, *Annals* 2.8, 11). Cohorts of Batavian infantry were also raised. Eight were to be stationed in Britain, no doubt from the beginning of the Roman occupation in AD 43 (Tacitus, *Hist.* 1.59, 2.27, 66, 4.12).[5] They had won fame in Rome's German wars, Tacitus writes, 'and their glory was enhanced in Britain, after the cohorts were transferred there, which, under the ancient agreement, were commanded by the noblest of their own people'. Two of these officers are named in this passage, the brothers Julius Civilis and Claudius Paulus, both 'of royal descent' (*Hist.* 4.12-13).

If the Batavians supplied eight cohorts and a cavalry *ala* and – up till 68 – contributed several hundred to the imperial bodyguard at Rome, a good 5000 Batavian males of military age were serving in the army at any one time. At this period, furthermore, auxiliaries could not look forward to any definite terminal point of their service. Discharge after 25 years was first introduced intermittently in the Flavian period and granted regularly only from Trajan's reign onwards.[6] Yet the Batavian territory in the Rhine-Maas delta was relatively small, and its total population has been calculated at no more than about 35,000. It looks as if at least one son from every family must have 'taken the Emperor's shilling'.[7]

The Batavian cohorts had been brigaded with the legion Fourteen Gemina in Britain and had certainly fought in the north of the island. A nephew of Civilis, also an officer in 70 – although actually commanding a *non*-Batavian cavalry regiment – was called Julius Briganticus (Tacitus, *Hist.* 2.22, 4.70, 5.21). He surely got his name because his father had been involved in early forays into the Pennines, in Brigantian territory.[8] The XIVth legion and the eight Batavian cohorts were withdrawn from Britain by Nero in 66, to join a planned expedition to the Caucasus, which never materialised (*Hist.* 1.6, 2.27, 4.15). The eight cohorts were ordered back to Britain, presumably by Galba, but by the end of 68 had only got as far as the territory of the Lingones, on the edge of the Vosges (*Hist.* 1.59). For a time Civilis and Paulus had been under arrest before Nero's death. Paulus was executed, Civilis freed on Galba's orders, then arrested again (*Hist.* 4.13). Meanwhile Galba had dissolved the largely Batavian imperial bodyguard: under their commander, a freedman gladiator, Ti. Claudius Spiculus, they had held out for Nero to the bitter end (*Hist.* 2.5; Suetonius, *Galba* 12); and the men were presumably sent home.[9]

Soon after his coup d'état at Cologne in January 69 Vitellius had Civilis, 'who had so much influence among the Batavians', released, as he did not want 'to alienate his warlike people' (*Hist.* 1.59, 2.27, 4.13). The Batavian cohorts soon caused trouble all the same, and began to attack the legionary troops (1.64), but fought with the Vitellians against Otho in April (2.17, 2.27); when they were ordered to be diverted to southern Gaul, the Vitellian troops protested 'if the high point of victory turned on Italy, the Batavians should not be detached from their forces: that would be like amputating a body's strongest limbs' (2.28). They duly took part in the decisive battle of Bedriacum (2.43).

After this Vitellian victory, the Batavians again showed lack of discipline, at Augusta Taurinorum (Turin), where their bad relations with the XIVth legion broke out into open fighting (2.66). Vitellius decided 'to send them back to Germany, in case they dared to create further disturbances' (2.69). The Roman commander in the Rhineland, Hordeonius Flaccus, regarded the Batavians as suspect (2.97). When news of Vespasian's bid for power in the east – supported by some of the Danube legions – reached the west, Vitellius began conscripting new troops, including in the Batavian country, which was contrary to the old agreement and aroused great resentment (*Hist.* 4.14). Civilis, who had already been canvassed to support Vespasian (4.13), took this as an excuse to rebel against Vitellius. The great uprising known as the Batavian Revolt thus began, ostensibly at least, as an action by anti-Vitellian troops in favour of Vespasian – who was claimed by Civilis to be his personal friend (*Hist.* 5.26): no doubt the two had fought together in Britain in the years 43-47, when Vespasian was legate of II Augusta.[10] Whatever the true motives, the revolt soon turned into an anti-Roman independence movement, in which a good many other northern peoples as well as the Batavi, from both sides of the frontier, took part, including the Tungri (*Hist.* 4.16, 66). Civilis was a frightening figure: he had lost an eye during his 25 years in Rome's service (*Hist.* 4.32) and when the revolt broke out he let his hair grow long and dyed it red (4.61).

After some striking rebel successes, the revolt was suppressed, by Vespasian's son-in-law Petillius Cerialis, with a force of 16 legions, as Tacitus describes in his *Histories*. This work breaks off in mid-sentence (5.26), with Petillius and Civilis negotiating on an island somewhere in the Rhine delta, in the early autumn of 70. It is plausible to suppose that in return for handing over their arms, the Batavians were granted a pardon (already offered to Civilis personally, 5.24) and the continuation of their old privileges, including the right to supply soldiers instead of taxes and for them to be recruited and commanded by their own aristocracy. Rome could not dispense with these crack troops.[11] Petillius probably took reconstituted Batavian regiments with him when he moved on to become governor of Britain.

Some Batavian aristocrats had stayed loyal to Rome, including two cavalry commanders, Claudius Labeo, prefect of the Batavian *ala*, and young Briganticus (*Hist.* 4. 66, 70; 5.21). It is a plausible inference that Petillius rewarded those among the elite who were not yet Roman citizens with this status, and that they assumed the family name of the new Emperor, Flavius. One of them, it may be further inferred, gave his son, born perhaps shortly afterwards, the *cognomen* of his benefactor: he would be called Flavius Cerialis. Just over a quarter of a century later, probably aged about 30, he was to command the Ninth Cohort of Batavians at Vindolanda.[12] Flavius Cerialis is the person most frequently recorded in the writing-tablets.

The Tungrians

The name of the other people who supplied a cohort for Vindolanda, the Tungri, survives in the Belgian town Tongeren or Tongres, the ancient Atuatuca Tungrorum, north of Liège. The Tungri are not mentioned by Caesar in his account of how he invaded Belgic Gaul, but he names 'Aduatuca' as a stronghold of the Eburones. This was one of the peoples to whom he gives a collective name, *Germani Cisrhenani*, 'Germans on the near side of the Rhine'. These also included the Condrusi (*BG* 6.2, cf. 2.4, 4.6, 6.32), a name which, in the adjectival form Condrustis, later crops up for a canton (*pagus*) of the Tungri (*RIB* 2108). The Tungri, as geographical sources show, lived on both sides of the River Meuse, in the territory once occupied by the *Germani Cisrhenani*. They were thus south-western neighbours of the Batavians. Tacitus supplies a – much debated – report about the Tungri:

> the name *Germania* is said to be a new and recent application: it was because the ones who first crossed the Rhine and expelled the Gauls, and are now called Tungri, were called *Germani* at that time. Thus, it is said, what was the name of one people, not of the whole nation, gradually acquired a wider usage: the conqueror, through fear, applied it to them all, and in due course, once they had got to know the name, they all called themselves *Germani*. (*Germany* 2.2).

Presumably 'Tungri' was the name (of uncertain meaning) applied under Augustus to the reconstituted remnants of the *Germani Cisrhenani*, who had suffered crippling losses against Caesar (*BG* 6.31ff.). At first the Tungri were in the province Gallia Belgica. When Domitian reorganised the military districts of the Rhineland into provinces, they were attached to Lower Germany.[13]

The reorganised *civitas* must have contained inhabitants of Gallic as well as Germanic origin, and the Germans were probably already considerably 'Celticised' at the time of the Roman occupation. Like all the peoples in northern Gaul and the Rhineland, the Tungri soon furnished auxiliary regiments to the Roman army. At least one of their units joined the Batavian revolt (*Hist.* 4.16) and the whole people soon, if only briefly, went over to the rebels (4.66, 79). When it was over, the First and Second Cohorts of Tungrian infantry and a cavalry *ala* were to serve in Britain, the *ala* from at least AD 98 until the mid-second century, the cohorts for several hundred years.[14]

The auxiliary regiments and their commanders

There were several distinct categories of 'auxiliary regiments', 'native' or 'colonial' troops recruited from Rome's subject peoples. Most 'junior' were the infantry cohorts, *cohortes peditatae*, known as 'quingenary', '500-strong', in practice only 480, divided into six centuries of 80 men, each with a centurion. By the second century AD the army had nearly 300 quingenary cohorts. A proportion of them – the *cohortes equitatae* – had an extra contingent, 120 cavalrymen, divided into four squadrons, *turmae*, each under a decurion. 'Quingenary' cohorts were all commanded by prefects (except for the handful recruited from Roman citizens, who were placed under tribunes). These men were all *equites Romani*, often translated 'Roman knights', in other words members of the equestrian order, second in the Roman hierarchy after the Senate.

In the early empire a graded career had developed, the 'three militias', *tres militiae*. But 'equestrian officers' were not professional soldiers. Most were from the 'gentry', local landowning elites, initially in Italy and the Roman colonies, and owed their appointment to the governor of the province in which they served. Often young men in their late teens or early twenties gained a commission, and cases are known of equestrian officers in their forties or even older. The largest single group was of men in their early thirties. Whatever their age on appointment, many returned to civilian life after a single tour of duty of about three years. Some had several successive appointments as prefect of a cohort.

The talented, the ambitious or the well-connected could continue upwards. From prefect of a cohort, he could be promoted to tribune of a legion, each of which had five equestrians in this post – or to be tribune commanding a double-strength cohort; a number of these began to be formed in the second half of the first century AD. These so-called 'milliary' or '1000-man strong' cohorts had 10 centuries of 80 men each, making their real strength only 800. But, again, some were *cohortes equitatae*, with a detachment of 240 cavalry, giving a total strength of 1040. The third *militia* involved the command as prefect of an entirely cavalry regiment, an *ala*, the exact size of which is not certain, but was perhaps 480, subdivided into 16 *turmae* of 30 men, each commanded by a decurion. A tiny handful of cavalry regiments – never more than ten in the whole empire – was 'doubled' in size and called *alae milliariae*, although in practice only about 800-strong.[15] Anomalously, the commanders of the Tungrian and Batavian cohorts continued to have the title 'prefect' instead of 'tribune' even after these regiments had become 'milliary'. Speculation (or reasoned conjecture) is possible as to the reason.[16]

On the face of it, the regimental commanders were divided by a great social gulf from their men. They lived in a large house, *praetorium*, in the central part of the fort, accompanied by wife and children, slaves and freedmen. Their salary was a good 50 times that paid to the ordinary soldiers[17] who occupied cramped sleeping and living quarters, two rooms shared by each *contubernium* of eight men. Centurions and their cavalry equivalents the decurions were better paid, of course, and their accommodation was more spacious, a two-room apartment at the end of the barrack-block. But they were mostly non-

32 The address of the letter to a double-pay man (312)

citizens like the soldiers from whose ranks they had generally been promoted. A large variety of what might be called 'non-commissioned officers' and higher-grade special-ists, known collectively as *principales*, can be identified. Apart from anything else, the latter received higher pay than the common soldiers.[18] An example from the writing tablets is a man called Cessaucius Nigrinus, who received a letter (312) at Vindolanda. He is described on the address as *dup(licarius)*, 'double-pay' man – but not all specialists were *principales*; some were simply *immunes*, 'exempted' from mundane tasks.

Some examples of *principales* and *immunes* are known from the Vindolanda tablets. Each centurion had a deputy, the *optio*, and alongside the decurion served a man with the title *curator*, perhaps the next senior within each *turma* and responsible for horses and their equipment. The letter from the decurion Masclus (1544) finally showed that the Ninth Batavians were already a part-mounted cohort when at Vindolanda. Regimental doctors, *medici*, and medical orderlies, *seplasiarii*, literally 'ointment-men', have clearly identifiable functions, likewise the vets, *veterinarii*, essential to care for the horses, transport-animals, oxen and mules, and for a whole range of livestock belonging to the regiment. The *cornicen*, horn-blower, had obvious duties, while the *tesserarius* was in charge of the *tessera*, token, with the watchword of the day – he seems to have ranked third in the century or squadron after the centurion or decurion and their respective deputies. The *beneficiarius*, literally, a man serving 'through the favour' (of the prefect, in this case), could represent his CO in a variety of functions; the

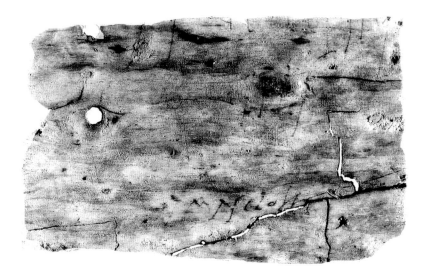

33 Inv. 1544R: 'From Masclus the decurion'

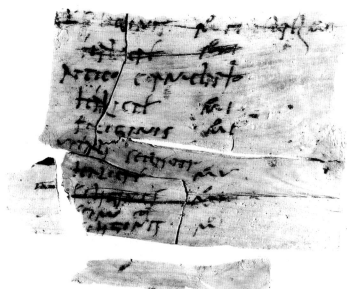

34 Inv. 1495: Atticus the cornicularius (line 3) and Vitalis the seplasiarius (line 6)

cornicularius, whose title referred originally to a small horn attached to his helmet, was the senior 'pen-pusher' in charge of the commander's office. At least one *signifer*, standard-bearer, is recorded, likewise a *vexillarius*, flag-bearer, who carried the *vexillum* of a detachment when it was away from its parent unit. Certain other labels attached to soldiers refer to their duties, although probably not involving any extra pay or status: Lucius the *scutarius*, 'shield-maker'; Tullio the *carpentarius*, 'wagon-man'; Vitalis the *balniator*, 'baths-man'; and Atrectus the *cervesarius*, 'brewer'.[19]

3 Vindolanda

Vindolanda lies almost exactly halfway between the North Sea and the Solway Firth, each some 60km distant, to the east and west. It occupies an escarpment or plateau, sharply defined on its south side by a small stream, the Doe Sike, which flows into the Chineley Burn on the east of the plateau. This is formed by the confluence, just below the north-eastern corner of the later stone fort, of two other streams, the Brackies or Cockton Burn coming from the north-west and the Bradley Burn from the north-east. The Chineley Burn itself flows into the River South Tyne about 1km to the south. Just over 0.5km east of Vindolanda towers the heather and bracken-covered Barcombe Hill, along the ridge of which stone quarries, exploited by the garrison,[1] still show up prominently. The east-west Roman road, the Stanegate, ran past the fort's northern rampart. Beyond it the ground rises markedly, up to the rugged north-facing crags of the Whin Sill, 1.5km distant, along which Hadrian's Wall was later to be constructed. Only to the west of Vindolanda is the ground level; and on this side there are plentiful springs, ensuring a regular water-supply. The internal lay-out of the Tungrians' early fort is not known, but that of the Batavians,

35 Vindolanda from the south

at least, faced west. From its west gate, then, the *via praetoria* ran east to join the north-south *via principalis*. Opposite the road-junction the headquarters building, *principia*, was erected, to the south of the *principia* the massive commanding officer's residence, *praetorium*.

The fort's name is Celtic: *vindos* meant 'white' or 'shining', and it survives as Welsh *gwyn* and Irish *finn*, as well as in the word *win*ter, the 'white season'. Several other place-names in Britain began *Vindo-*: Vindobala (Rudchester) and Vindomora (Ebchester), also Roman forts, are examples close to Vindolanda, and Vindogara was a native settlement in Ayrshire. Vindobona on the Danube (modern Vienna) and Vindonissa (near Brugg in Switzerland) are well-known sites on the Continent, both housing legionary fortresses. *Landa* meant 'enclosure' or 'lawn', from the same root as Welsh *llan*.[2] One can guess why the place got the name: soon after sunrise in winter, the plateau stays in the shadow cast by Barcombe after the frost all round has melted: for half an hour or so it really does look like a 'shining enclosure' or 'white lawn'. The name must already have existed when the Romans first saw Vindolanda, in the early 70s. No trace of a British settlement has yet been detected. It is likely that there was at least a holy place there: the Celts attached sacred significance to springs, streams and rivers.[3] The watersmeet at Vindolanda would have been an ideal location for a shrine or sacred grove.

One name of a British people is attested, by an altar found 3km away, at Beltingham on the far side of the River S. Tyne (*RIB* 1695). It was dedicated to the goddess Saitada, by the *curia Textoverdorum*. Carving, language (*deae* and the formula *VSLM*) and lettering are Roman enough. *Curia* in Latin means 'senate-house' or, by extension, 'assembly'; but here it might be a variant for the postulated Celtic word *coria*, 'hosting-place'. But *-xt-* in Textoverdi is a 'native' usage: in Gaul *x* had been borrowed from Greek *chi* for the guttural Celtic *ch* (as in Welsh *bach* and Scottish *loch*). Romans generally ignored the difference and used *c*, as with the Tectosages of Gaul and Galatia. Saitada is totally unknown elsewhere. Her name is thought to mean 'goddess of grief', which would associate her with funerary rites. Whatever may be inferred from this stone – which could indeed have been taken to Beltingham from Vindolanda itself in post-Roman times – it looks second- or third- century in style.[4]

For the Vindolanda garrison and their Roman contacts, apparently, the local natives were undifferentiated, just *Brittones*. They are referred to as such in two writing tablets. One, from a Period II level (1108), is neutral: it is a letter about supply, and mentions 'wagons of the *Brittones*' bringing corn to the garrison. In the other (164), from a Period III level, the inadequacy of the *Brittones* at using weapons is described, and they are given a derogatory nickname, *Brittunculi*, 'little Brits'. Presumably British conscripts were being trained at Vindolanda. The Anavionenses of Annandale, whose territory stretched down to the north side of the Solway, are named in a fragmentary Period III tablet (1475); it seems likely that the scornful label *Brittunculi* referred to them. It is not known which British people ruled the land around Vindolanda itself when the Romans first arrived: perhaps it was the Textoverdi. The Brigantes, the largest *civitas* in Britain, whose territory stretched from sea to sea, occupied most of the Pennines; but the northernmost part of

36 *The Brittones supply grain (Inv. 1108). Brittonum is written at the end of the fourth
line of the left-hand sheet; just to the right of this and a line higher on the other sheet is
the word Vindolanda*

England probably lay outside their control.[5] In the north-west, present-day Cumbria,
were the Carvetii, whose territory included Luguvalium, and no doubt Edenside and
Stainmore as well. The Votadini inhabited Northumberland and much of south-
eastern Scotland. To their west, in upper Tweeddale, were the Selgovae, in whose
territory was the three-peaked stronghold after which the Romans called their
nearby fort Trimontium (Newstead). The neighbours of the Selgovae on the other
side were the Anavionenses. Somewhere east of Vindolanda there was at least one
other people. They are known only from an altar (*RIB* 1142, found in Hexham
Abbey, presumably brought there from Corbridge) dedicated by a Roman officer,
'after slaughtering a band of Corionotatae'.[6]

A few native settlements are known close to Vindolanda. On top of the north end
of Barcombe was a small British hill-fort. There can be no doubt that occupation
here ceased at the latest when the Roman army arrived in the area: a Roman signal
station was built inside it. A few hundred metres north of this, at Crindledykes, a
native farmstead has been identified by air photography. Another, consisting of five
round stone huts, was at Milking Gap, just over 1km due north of Vindolanda on
the southern slopes of the Whin Sill. It was evidently abandoned when Hadrian's
Wall and its attendant works engulfed it.[7]

Vindolanda was not quite 'on the edge of empire' when the Tungrians built their
fort or when the Ninth Batavians followed them here. Much of southern Scotland,
including Annandale and the Borders, was still occupied. Twenty years on, the with-
drawal of the Ninth Batavians from Vindolanda, which can be dated to summer 105,
was to be accompanied by the evacuation of most of the bases to its north. Other
units probably left at the same time, sharply reducing the size of the British garrison:
Trajan's Second Dacian war started in June that year, with Roman losses, and rein-
forcements were clearly required.[8] Even the Eburacum legion, IX Hispana, which
rebuilt one of the gateways of its fortress in 108 (*RIB* 665), may have been transferred
to the continent a few years later, to plug a gap, in this case after troops from the west

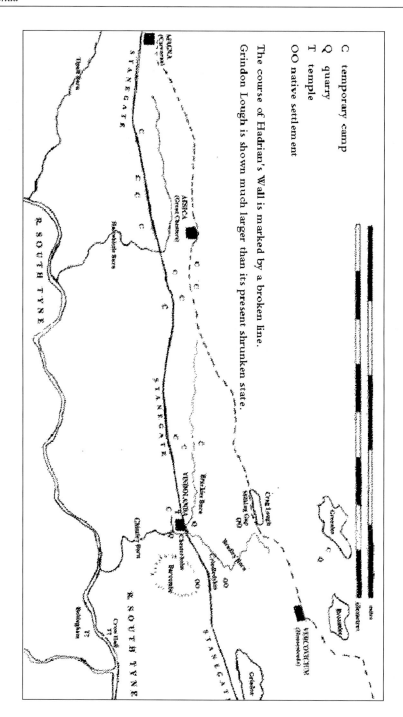

The following legend appears on the map:

C temporary camp
Q quarry
T temple
OO native settlement

The course of Hadrian's Wall is marked by a broken line.
Grindon Lough is shown much larger than its present shrunken state.

37 *Map 2: the Vindolanda area*

38   Vindolanda from the air: view from the north

39   View of Barcombe Hill from Vindolanda

were moved to the eastern frontier for the Parthian War, which began in 113.[9] From 105 onwards, then, the Vindolanda garrison may be regarded as part of a 'frontier force', at least until the reoccupation of Scotland *c.*AD 140. The nature of this frontier can be variously described. The main Roman road, the Stanegate, from Luguvalium, or better, from Kirkbride on the Solway, further west, to Coria, and the forts along it, were certainly a vital element. It is a question whether any kind of east-west frontier line extended east of Coria.[10] Rather, the Roman north road, Dere Street, going through Coria towards Scotland, if no longer as far as Trimontium, may effectively have marked the limit of Roman control on the eastern side. East of this road lay the main part of the Votadinian territory: this apparently pro-Roman people would then still be defended against their western neighbours. In other words, the Stanegate and Dere Street, with the forts along these roads, formed a pincer-shaped system to contain any threat from north and west. The line along Dere Street from Coria at least to Habitancum (Risingham), and probably to Bremenium (High Rochester) as well, was later known as a *praetensio*, a 'line of manned points linking a rearward base to an outpost'.[11] What the position at these Dere Streets forts was in the Trajanic period is at present unknown: they have hardly been explored.

To the north of Vindolanda and in the high country beyond the South Tyne on the other side, the land is bleak and the moors suitable only for grazing and hunting deer, wild boar, hare and other game, especially birds. But in the South Tyne valley there was ample scope for agriculture. Initially the garrison was no doubt supplied by grain brought in from some distance. Before long wheat, barley and other cereals could have been obtained locally, including *bracis*, used for making beer. In close proximity to the fort, coal, clay, lead and ironstone could be worked. Further, there were several sources of easily worked sandstone or limestone, both in the valleys to the north-west and east of the fort and slightly further afield on Barcombe Hill.

The most important Roman bases on the Stanegate, Coria (Corbridge) and Luguvalium (Carlisle), are both mentioned in the tablets, the former very frequently – it was probably a major source of supply for Vindolanda. But the name of the main Roman base to the north, Trimontium (Newstead), evacuated *c.*105, does not occur. Bremenium (High Rochester) is only mentioned in an isolated later tablet, from the second half of the second century, at a time when it was an outpost beyond Hadrian's Wall. At any rate, there are plenty of references to bases to the south: Vinovia (Binchester), Cataractonium (Catterick), Isurium (Aldborough), Bremetennacum (Ribchester) and Eburacum (York) – and Londinium, no doubt already the 'capital' of the province and the principal residence of the governor. Lindum (Lincoln), for several decades a legionary base, which had acquired the status of a Roman *colonia* under Domitian, is perhaps also mentioned. Several other places named in the tablets have not yet been identified. Briga and Ulucium are likely to have been forts along the Stanegate. A probable location for Briga is Kirkbride west of Luguvalium, the true terminal point of this road. Ulucium could well be at Newbrough, between Vindolanda and Coria. But Cordonovi (or -a or -ae) was probably somewhere on the coast, perhaps even in the south of Britain or outside the province – it is mentioned as the source of oysters.[12]

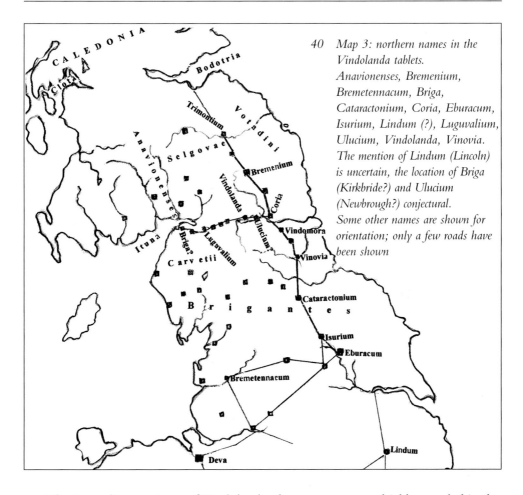

40 Map 3: northern names in the
Vindolanda tablets.
Anavionenses, Bremenium,
Bremetennacum, Briga,
Cataractonium, Coria, Eburacum,
Isurium, Lindum (?), Luguvalium,
Ulucium, Vindolanda, Vinovia.
The mention of Lindum (Lincoln)
is uncertain, the location of Briga
(Kirkbride?) and Ulucium
(Newbrough?) conjectural.
Some other names are shown for
orientation; only a few roads have
been shown

The immediate environs of Vindolanda, then as now, were thickly wooded in the valley to the east of the fort. Beech, birch, alder, willow, oak and hazel trees grew in profusion. Both building timber and firewood were close to hand – and, indeed, the raw material for making leaf writing tablets. In Roman times this woodland probably extended south of the fort. Barcombe Hill would certainly have been carpeted with heather and bracken. Given the large quantities of bracken used as flooring in the fort, its harvesting must have been a regular activity – to cover 30m square at least one hectare of bracken would have had to be cut.[13] Once the fort was well established, in the Batavian period, a visitor coming from the east on the road from Coria (the direction with the best view of the site) would have seen the massive ramparts, topped by a palisade, of the playing-card shaped fort, with its rounded corners; within the ramparts rows of barracks with streets running between them; and in the centre some particularly substantial buildings, granaries, a hospital (*valetudinarium*), the commander's residence, *praetorium*, and headquarters, *principia*.

Outside the fort, at the south-east corner, stood the impressive stone bath-house. Close to this and beyond the western and northern ramparts there must have been wagon-parks, traders' huts and shops, workshops, great piles of coal and building materials – especially bricks and tiles, quarried stone and timber – charcoal burners' furnaces, tileries and all manner of 'industrial' activity. There would be lime-kilns down in the valley of the Chineley Burn, where limestone was quarried, and there was probably a mason's yard there too, where large blocks of stone from the quarry could be cut into more manageable pieces, easier to bring up the hill to the fort.[14] Smoke rising from all this activity and from the furnace that heated the bath-house would have been visible from a long way off. A temple beyond the western defences and next to the Stanegate, with a square inner *cella*, surrounded by an outer *temenos* wall, probably plastered and whitewashed, would have showed up conspicuously, the *cella* being like a square tower, up to 6m high. Further beyond would be farm animals grazing – horses, oxen, pigs, sheep and goats and poultry, both chickens and geese, the oxen in the woods, some of the other livestock certainly in pens or fenced enclosures or fields, to protect them against foxes, wolves and other predators. Stalls in which some of the beasts could find shelter in winter were surely also to be seen.

On the way to Vindolanda, birds would have been seen in profusion, and some heard: both small songbirds such as thrushes, and wood pigeons, curlews, peewits, kingfishers, herons and swans. Squirrels will have abounded. Coming closer, the visitor would have been aware of the noise: hammering and sawing, wagon-wheels trundling along the Stanegate, horses' hooves, cattle lowing, cocks crowing, dogs barking or howling – and of course human voices, women's as well as men's, speaking not only Latin, but quite probably a form of Celtic and even a Germanic language as well. From time to time trumpet or bugle calls would be heard, even the sound of marching feet, if the men were setting out for or returning from an exercise or patrol, or training on the parade ground. The visitor must also have noticed the smells of Roman Vindolanda, not least of tanning, smoke, horses and farm animals. Once inside the fort it would have been impossible not to be aware of the smell from the dried bracken and straw carpeting in most of the rooms and the yards outside them, in which all manner of debris was mixed. No one brought up on a farm (as most members of the garrison undoubtedly were) would have wrinkled their noses at any of this.[15] At certain times of day there would also have been noticeable smells of cooking, from the numerous bread-ovens and from various stews, heavily flavoured with garlic, fish-sauce, coriander and other spices.[16]

4 Tungrians, Batavians and Tungrians again

Petillius Cerialis as Governor of Britain

When the Emperor Claudius left Britain after his brief stay of 16 days in summer 43, he instructed the commander-in-chief of his expeditionary force, Aulus Plautius, 'to conquer the rest' (Dio 60.21.5). How well informed the Romans were about the extent of the island is not clear. At all events, by 68 the new province would encompass England up to the southern Pennines and some of Wales. The attempt to complete the conquest of North Wales had had to be abandoned on the outbreak of Boudicca's rebellion in 60 and was not to be completed for over 15 years. Indirect control was exercised over the Brigantes of the Pennines, the largest single people in Britain: their queen regnant Cartimandua was a subservient client of Rome – she had handed over the resistance leader Caratacus when he sought refuge. But her ex-husband Venutius, whom she had divorced in favour of his armour-bearer, took the opportunity afforded by the Year of the Four Emperors, 69, to oust the 'quisling queen', hated by the Brigantes 'on account of her cruelty and lust' (Tacitus, *Hist.* 3.45). Large numbers of troops had been withdrawn from a garrison already weakened by the transfer of legion XIV and the Batavian cohorts in 66. The governor Vettius Bolanus, newly installed in 69, was at least able to rescue Cartimandua and perhaps even to defeat Venutius. But the situation was fraught when his successor Petillius Cerialis arrived early in 71. He brought an extra legion with him, the newly founded II Adiutrix, to bring the legionary strength back up to four – joining II Augusta, IX Hispana and XX Valeria Victrix. IX Hispana, which he had himself commanded at the time of Boudicca's revolt, was now stationed in a new forward base, Eburacum. II Adiutrix occupied IX Hispana's old base at Lindum. Petillius had a clear mandate for a renewed forward policy from Vespasian.[1]

Tacitus' appraisal of Petillius' achievement is slightly grudging: he 'at once struck terror into the enemy by attacking the state of the Brigantes, reckoned to be the most populous in the whole province. There were many battles, some not without bloodshed; and he embraced a great part of the Brigantes within the range of either victory or war' (*Agr.* 17). Modern historians of Roman Britain were long reluctant to credit Petillius with an advance much further north than Scotch Corner, close to the Brigantian stronghold of Stanwick. But it is now known, through dendrochronology, that the first Roman fort at Luguvalium (Carlisle) was built during his governorship, with oak timbers from trees felled in the winter of 72/3.[2] Petillius had a further full season thereafter and surely penetrated into Scotland. The legate of the XXth legion under Petillius, who played a prominent part in his campaigns, was Gnaeus Julius Agricola (*Agr.* 5, 8). Agricola left Britain at the same time as Petillius, to be governor of Aquitania and then consul (*Agr.* 9).

The Governorship of Agricola

Petillius' successor, Sextus Julius Frontinus, devoted his attention principally to South Wales, as Tacitus indicates. At the time he was writing, Frontinus was one of the new Emperor Trajan's right-hand men, his colleague in the consulship of 98. It was probably better not to go into too much detail. Tacitus was flattering but brief: 'Julius Frontinus, a great man, in so far as it was then possible to be great, took up and sustained the burden; and he subjugated the strong and warlike people of the Silures, overcoming not merely the courage of the enemy but the difficulties of the terrain' (*Agr.* 17). By 'took up and sustained the burden' Tacitus probably implies that Frontinus continued the consolidation of the north as well as subjugating South Wales. When Agricola returned to Britain, in midsummer 77, to succeed Frontinus as governor, his first task, in the half-season that remained, was unfinished business in North Wales, where the Ordovices of Snowdonia had just attacked a Roman fort and practically wiped out a cavalry regiment.[3] He went on to capture the island of Mona (Anglesey), stronghold of the Druids (*Agr.* 18). In his second year, 78, he could turn his attention to the north, 'reconnoitring estuaries and forests personally' and 'giving the enemy no rest, by launching sudden plundering raids . . . As a result, many states which up to that moment had operated on equal terms abandoned violence and gave hostages. They were also surrounded by garrisons and forts, with such skill and thoroughness that no new part of Britain ever came over with so little damage' (*Agr.* 20).

Since Petillius had founded Luguvalium five years before, this second campaign of Agricola must have been in southern Scotland. His third, in 79, was directed against 'new peoples . . . in territories as far as the Taus [Tay]' (*Agr.* 22). During that summer the old Emperor Vespasian died, to be succeeded by his elder son Titus, probably a personal friend of Agricola, certainly his exact coeval. No doubt on the basis of Agricola's reports, Titus decided that enough had been achieved. Operations in 80 were devoted to consolidation along the Forth-Clyde line: here, 'if the spirit of the army and the glory of the Roman name had permitted it, a frontier had been found within Britain itself' (*Agr.* 23). In 81, Agricola turned to the furthest part of south-west Scotland, largely by-passed up until then, perhaps going as far as Kintyre, and drew up his army facing Ireland. He had with him an Irish minor king, who had sought refuge, 'treating him like a friend, and keeping him in case an opportunity arose'. Later, Tacitus recalls, 'I often heard Agricola say that Ireland could be conquered and held with a single legion and modest numbers of *auxilia*' (*Agr.* 24). Agricola's winter-quarters in these years were probably at Luguvalium, where a writing-tablet has registered the presence of one of his horse-guardsmen; and a few weeks after the battle of Mons Graupius men of the XXth legion were stationed there.[4]

A dramatic change of policy now occurred: in September 81 Titus suddenly died, aged only 41, and his younger brother Domitian succeeded. After years in the shadow of the conqueror of Jerusalem, Domitian was avid for military glory. Eighteen months later he was to lead his own massive expedition, intended to annexe large tracts of Germany beyond the Upper Rhine and Upper Danube.[5] As for Britain, expansion was once again the policy: Agricola was to conquer the whole island. Its true extent had at last become clear. It was not after all shaped 'like an axe or an elongated shoulder-blade', as previously thought. 'That is indeed what it looks like on this side of Caledonia. Those who have gone past this [that is, Agricola and his men] have found a huge and irregular expanse of land, projecting beyond the apparently outermost shore and tapering into a wedge-like shape' (*Agr.* 10).

The average tenure of office of Agricola's ten predecessors had been less than four years. He had already been there for five, but no doubt persuaded Domitian that one last season would do the trick. The sixth season began with a push beyond the Forth and with the fleet being involved for the first time. But the northern Britons were far from beaten: they launched a dangerous counter-attack against the Ninth legion (*Agr.* 25-8). Still another year was needed. The details of Agricola's advance in 83 to Mons Graupius, at 'the furthest end of the island' (*Agr.* 30, 33) are only indirectly given, in the speech Tacitus gives Agricola before the battle. It had involved crossing 'marshes, mountains and rivers . . . forests and estuaries and gorges' (*Agr.* 33-4). It was late September ('summer was already over', *Agr.* 38).

The great battle, in which the auxiliaries, 8000 infantry and 3000 cavalry, bore the brunt of the fighting on the Roman side, with the four Batavian and two Tungrian cohorts singled out for special mention, ended in complete victory: 10,000 Britons dead, only 360 Romans (*Agr.* 35-8). But it was followed at once by Agricola's recall. Domitian's own campaign of 83 had achieved much less than it had seemed to promise and – so Tacitus portrays it – the Emperor was jealous of his general's genuine success (*Agr.* 39f.). All the same, 'Britain was completely conquered' (Tacitus, *Agr.* 10; *Hist.* 1.2), and one of the four legions was given a new forward base on the River Tay, at Inchtuthil. Forts were established to block the Highland glens, and by now much of southern Scotland and northern England was likewise garrisoned.

The first known fort at Vindolanda

The occupation of the far north was only to last a few years. Shortly after Agricola left, a series of military disasters afflicted Rome's forces on the Danube (*Agr.* 41; *Hist.* 1.2) and the large numbers of seasoned troops in Britain had to be called upon to make good the losses. The legion II Adiutrix and several auxiliary regiments, including at least two of the Batavian cohorts, I and II, were transferred to serve in Pannonia and Moesia; the other two, the Third and Ninth, were retained. The Inchtuthil fortress, which had never quite been completed, was dismantled and the forts north of the Forth-Clyde line evacuated.[6] Wherever the First Cohort of Tungrians had been serving, it was now sent to Vindolanda.

Agricola had evidently had his headquarters for a time at Luguvalium (Carlisle).[7] Either he or one of his predecessors, Petillius and Julius Frontinus, could have ordered a fort to be built at Vindolanda, one might imagine. But no material from the 70s or early 80s has yet been found there – the earliest samian belongs to the years just after Agricola, *c.*85-92. Possibly there was an original fort on the north side of the later east-west Roman road, the Stanegate.[8] At present, nothing is known of the site before the Tungrians arrived.

They are the earliest attested garrison at Vindolanda, as revealed by a stylus tablet (Inv. 787) containing the regiment's name, *c(o)ho(rtis) Tung(rorum)*, in the address and by a remarkable ink tablet (154), a 'strength report'.[9] They were found in the innermost western ditch of the fort. Other finds from here, especially samian in large quantities, are datable *c.*85-92. This ditch, at least 4.5m wide and a little over 1.5m deep, was the first of a series defending the western side of the fort, probably at least six. There cannot have been so many ditches on the north, where the ground in any case falls away towards the Brackies Burn. To the east, the steep slope down to the Chineley Burn would surely have made more than one or two ditches unnecessary. One has been found on the south,

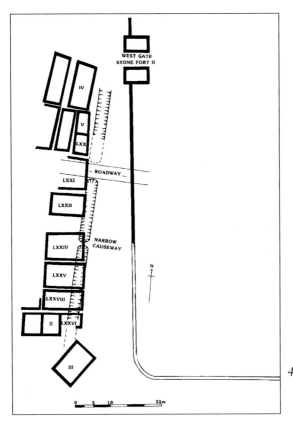

41   *The Period I innermost western ditch in relation to the west wall of the later stone fort*

which at one stage was filled in, but then re-cut, but there is no sign of further ditches: the ground also slopes away here, down to the Doe Sike.[10] The massive defences on the exposed western side suggest that at some stage there was a threat of attack.

When the Tungrians built their fort the cohort was probably of standard size, 480 men, all infantry. The estimated space available, *c.*1.4ha (3.5 acres), is the norm for such a unit. Only pottery supplies dating evidence, but this is pretty conclusive. There are virtually no examples of the samian Form 29, well represented in early Flavian forts in Scotland. By contrast, over 60 different pottery vessels assignable to the latest, 'decadent' phase of the South Gaulish production centre at La Graufesenque, many almost complete except for a small rim section, and apparently unused, had been dumped in the ditch. Clearly the consignment had been damaged in transit and thrown out. Another unsatisfactory delivery had already landed in the ditch – a profusion of oyster shells, many unbroken, their contents presumably found to be unfit to eat, lay under-neath the dumped samian. Not much was found above the samian, apart from a wooden needle case, a tent peg, a leather saddle cover – and writing tablets.[11] A small part of the southern rampart and ditch of the Tungrians' first fort has also been examined. The southern ditch, originally nearly 4m wide and 1.45m deep, slightly less substantial than the western inner ditch, was at some stage filled in with stone, either because a ditch on this side seemed superfluous or because another one was dug further out. However, it was then re-cut in the northern half, producing a new ditch 1.8m wide at the top and just over 1m deep. Finds included a worn coin of Vespasian, a horse's skull, industrial slag, a fragment of an iron pen nib with part of its wooden shaft, several wooden objects and various leather scraps, including a piece of a woman's shoe.[12]

The figures on the strength report give a total of 752 men, almost the size of a double, 'milliary' infantry cohort, 800 – but only 296 soldiers were present at Vindolanda, the remaining 456 absent at various places. It is plausible that the regiment was in the course of being increased in size – it is first attested as milliary in January 103, but could have reached this size well before. 337 absentees were 'at Coria'. Perhaps they were new recruits, being trained.[13] If so, when they were ready to join the regiment, the Vindolanda fort would be too small: they would have to rebuild or move elsewhere. Meanwhile, having a garrison only 60 per cent of the strength of a normal cohort could have prompted the prefect to have the extra ditches dug on the exposed western side.

An anomalous feature of the two Tungrian cohorts stationed in Britain must be recalled: even after they had been doubled in size, their commanders continued to be called 'prefect', not 'tribune' which was the normal title of rank for commanders of 'milliary' cohorts. The reason could be that members of the Tungrian aristocracy had previously been given this title in the homeland, as *praefecti civitatis*, administering their people for Rome. If the commanders of the Tungrian regiments were also Tungrian nobles, as seems probable, they may have insisted on retaining the title 'prefect'. A similar situation may be detected in the case of the Batavians.[14]

Soon after AD 90 it was decided that Vindolanda needed not only a larger fort but a different type of regiment, with cavalry. The Tungrians left – destination unknown, but still somewhere in Britain, it seems, and probably not very far away – and were replaced by the Ninth Batavians.[15] Unlike the First Tungrians, the Ninth Batavians were a mixed regiment, mainly infantry, but with a cavalry section, a *cohors equitata*; although this is not certain, in all probability it was already a double-cohort, as was the case a few years later, after it had left Britain.[16] In other words, it would have had 800 infantry and 240 cavalry and would have needed a much larger fort, including stabling for the horses. The commanders of the Batavian milliary cohorts, like those of the Tungrians, continued to be prefects rather than tribunes, as is known from later inscriptions from other provinces.[17] Thus the fact that the commanders of the Ninth Batavians at Vindolanda are all prefects does not mean that the regiment was only '500' strong. It may be noted that the Ninth's sister-unit, the Third Batavians, was evidently based somewhere in the vicinity, probably at a fort called Ulucium (311, cf. 174), not securely identified but perhaps Newbrough, only 11km east along the Stanegate, on the way to Coria.[18]

The Batavians at Vindolanda

The 'Batavian period', *c.*90/92-105 (Periods II–III), saw the remodelling and enlargement of the fort. At an estimated 2.8ha (7 acres) it was twice the size of its Tungrian predecessor. The Tungrians' ditches were filled in; the Batavians had to build on top of them. This applied to barracks, in part of the fort, above the outer ditches. But even part of the new central range, including the prefect's house, *praetorium*, had to be constructed over the innermost western ditch of the old fort. The new *via principalis* ran north to south along the short side of the fort, past the west front of the *praetorium*, over the outer lip of the old inner ditch, which at its southern end is at the lowest point of the plateau. Water from springs to the west flows naturally this way, down to the Doe Sike. Not surprisingly, repeated attempts were made, then and later, to create a dry surface: the depression was filled with large whinstone boulders, tree-trunks, wattle-fencing and crushed stone, topped by puddled clay. But these had only limited success. However, the circumstances – damp material sealed by clay – were to create ideal anaerobic conditions, helping to preserve organic material that would normally have perished. The new southern rampart, about 4.5m wide at its base, was of turf, in layers interspersed with horizontal timber strapping. Its gate passage had a single portal, some 3.25m wide, with timber posts, the threshold formed by a single beam of alder wood. The roadway inside the fort was paved with a raft of split logs, lying north to south, above a layer of turf and clay. There had clearly been major subsidence, for the gate was built over a natural gulley (down which water still flows). A wattle drain was inserted to channel this water beneath the portal, the gulley bridged with a solid frame at the gate passage and a raft of heavy logs pegged into place further north, at the road junction.[19]

East of the gate passage ran the intervallum road, over 6.5m wide. On its north side was a large building, identifiable as the prefect's house, *praetorium*. The west front, divided into over a dozen separate rooms, with a courtyard on their inner side, was 45.75m long. Construction of this Period II building was clearly hasty and flimsy.

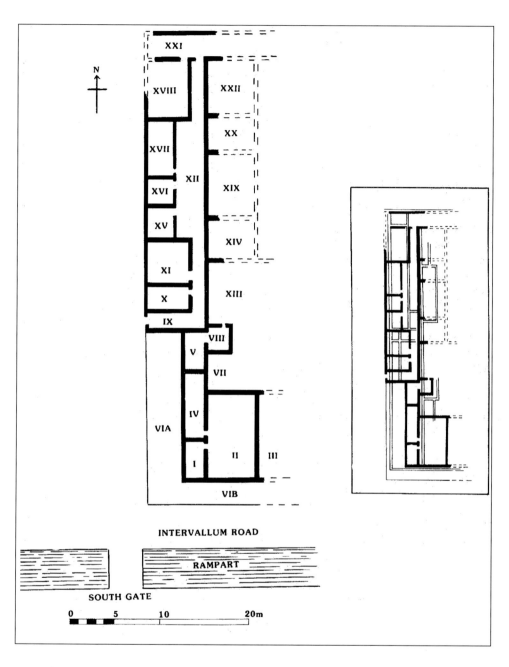

42　Plan of the praetorium in Period III with, inset, its position above its Period II predecessor

*43   The buckled threshold of the Period II south gate in the background, in foreground
timber strapping supporting the roadway over the natural gully*

Substantial circular posts had been used for the outer loadbearing walls and squared
posts for the main north-south inner wall, but the main uprights in the rooms were
mostly logs of birch or alder, set in the ground with the bark still on them. All the
partition walls were of wattle and daub with no base-beams, the floors of beaten clay,
with stone used only for a hearth. An unusual feature was a large water-tank, 1.25m
deep, 10.75m long and over 3m wide, in the courtyard, alongside the corridor, outside
a room near the northern end of the building. Adjacent to the tank considerable
debris from industrial activity was found, including a thick spread of coal dust and
charcoal, pieces of crucibles, fragments of iron and lead, bronze waste and slag.

Most of the rooms had a 'carpet' made of layers of bracken, straw and mosses, its thickness ranging from 1 to 32cm. Clearly the intention was to counteract the damp. Everywhere in the building – except in the water-tank – were found pieces of textile, discarded shoes, and leather offcuts indicating the repair of tents and saddlery. They were all preserved by the combination of damp conditions and the organic material in the bracken and straw 'carpets' in which they were thrown away. All were sealed when a rebuild was ordered (Period III). The rubbish accumulated in these 'carpets' may have generated a powerful smell, especially where leather was being processed, involving the use of urine. The people who lived – or rather worked – there no doubt got used to it; and the bracken perhaps helped a little.[20]

The nature of these finds might suggest that the building was a workshop, *fabrica*. But over 60 writing tablets, both stylus and leaf, were also found, a good many from correspondence of the prefects. Further, the building was replaced by one of similar design which was unquestionably the prefect's residence. It may be supposed that the industrial activity was carried out either by slaves in the prefect's household or by soldiers with specialist skills. The prefect and his family no doubt had their living and dining quarters well away from this industrial activity, in other wings of the building.[21]

That the unit in garrison in Period II was the Ninth Batavians is confirmed by two writing tablets. One (282) has in the address *[coh] VIIII Bat(avorum)* (*Bat* being very faint), the other (396) just *c(o)hor(tis) VIIII*, but this can only be the Ninth Batavians. Another fragmentary tablet (136) from Period II, although it does not preserve the name or number of the regiment, is one of the reports, *renuntia*, in many other examples of which this cohort is named (see next chapter). Further confirmation is supplied by a piece of cow hide found in silt at the bottom of the water-tank, neatly stamped CIXB, *c(ohortis) IX B(atavorum)*.[22] (In the tablets VIIII rather than IX was used virtually without exception to write 9.)

Evidence for the Ninth Batavians still being there in Period III is very considerable. A stylus tablet (Inv. 725) dated 19 January AD 98 from this level suggests (though it does not prove) that this period had begun at latest in the previous year. But Period III has supplied the majority of the writing tablets, including dozens of letters and documents relating to the prefect of the Ninth, Flavius Cerialis, clearly in office at the end of the Batavians' stay at Vindolanda, probably from 101-105, and to his wife Sulpicia Lepidina – and their friends and correspondents. A draft letter (225) written by Cerialis mentions as governor of Britain Neratius Marcellus, known to have been in office on 19 January AD 103,[23] and a document (1474A) found with rubbish discarded when the Batavians left contains consular dates at least for 103 and 104, and probably for 102 as well (see chapter 7).

Any insecurity, implied by the Tungrians' multiple ditches, had clearly been dispelled during the Batavians' occupation. At any rate, outside the western end of their fort a temple was constructed. It was built of soft yellow sandstone from the quarry closest to the fort, up the valley of the Brackies Burn. The design is typical of those in the north-western, Celtic provinces: a rectangular inner shrine, *cella*, measuring just over 5m from east to west by 3.5m north to south, surrounded by an ambulatory or outer wall, 9.65m x 8.5m. The door in the south side of the *cella* was crafted from a single block of grey limestone.[24] A small altar found outside the temple, 35cm high, shows that the shrine was dedicated to a god (rather than a goddess): the first line can be read as DEO. What survives in the remaining two lines is very worn, but it may be that the name is that of the chief god of the Batavians, Magusanus.[25]

While the Batavians were improving their fort at Vindolanda, at the end of Period II and the start of Period III, major developments had been taking place at the centre of the empire – and in the German provinces: Domitian was assassinated on 18 September 96 and was replaced by the 60-year-old Marcus Cocceius Nerva.[26] Lacking military connections, Nerva was in a dangerous position. The army had been devoted to Domitian – who had awarded the first pay increase in 130 years. At Rome in October the next year, the Praetorian Guard mutinied: Nerva, besieged in the palace, saved himself by sacrificing Domitian's killers to a lynch party. He insured against future hostile action from the troops by adopting a strong military man as son and heir: M. Ulpius Traianus – Trajan – whom he had just installed as governor of Upper Germany.[27]

Trajan, now 'Traianus Caesar', moved his headquarters from Moguntiacum (Mainz) to the Colonia Agrippinensis (Cologne) in Lower Germany. Nerva expired only three months later: on 28 January 98, Trajan became emperor. He remained in the Rhineland for some time. One of his first measures was to recruit a new horse guard, once again favouring Batavians for this elite unit. Like their predecessors, the *corpore custodes* of the Julio-Claudians, these Horse Guardsmen, whose official title was the *equites singulares Augusti*, were also nicknamed 'the Batavians'.[28] The new ruler's presence in their homeland thus gave the Batavians a chance to attract attention. Ambitious young men like Flavius Genialis and Flavius Cerialis were probably among them – Genialis may have gained his command over the Ninth Batavians from Trajan at this time.

Tacitus was meanwhile composing the biography of Agricola, his father-in-law, who had died in August 93, his achievements insufficiently recognised, Tacitus thought. But if he hoped that Trajan would order the reoccupation of what Agricola had conquered in northern Britain, he must have been disappointed. Trajan gave Britain a low priority: the choice, probably in 101 at the latest, of Lucius Neratius Marcellus as governor – a man lacking experience of military command – is one reflection of this. All the same, Marcellus' father, uncle and brother all had extensive service with the army. His brother Priscus governed Lower Germany soon after Trajan left the area. Flavius Cerialis seems to have arrived to take over command of the Ninth Batavians at Vindolanda in early summer 101. Perhaps Priscus had recommended him to Marcellus.[29]

This all remains speculation. At far off Vindolanda, events at Rome and in the Rhineland probably made little impact. There was work to be done – in the interests of the Batavians' own comfort. The main reason for the reconstruction was undoubtedly that the original gateway and *praetorium* were simply too flimsy.[30] How much of the rest of the fort was also refurbished at the same time is not clear. Several writing

44 *The wooden floor of the corridor at the north end of the Period III praetorium, where it crossed the Period I ditch. It was covered with turf to counteract the subsidence: this concealed it from the demolition gang*

tablets show building work in progress in Period III, involving a bath-house, *balneum*, and hospital, *valetudinarium* (155), guest-house, *hospitium*, and wattle fences (156). The bath-house has been located, a little way beyond the fort's south-east corner. It was a fine stone building, nearly 30m long, with all the usual features: from vestibule and changing-room to cold, warm and hot rooms, the extra hot *laconicum*, cold plunge and latrine, as well as furnace and aqueduct. In the hot room (*caldarium*) the walls were plastered. The tiles used for the hypocaust pillars, probably made in kilns nearby, had been left in the open air to dry before firing. Many had animal-prints on them, especially of dogs' paws, but also of cats, cows, pigs and sheep or goats.[31]

The new Period III south gateway was set just over 2m west of its predecessor and built in a different style.[32] A pile of decomposing wall plaster found lying against the north side of the rampart suggests that the gatehouse had been rendered on the outside. The new *praetorium* extended 1.5m further to the west than its predecessor and at over 50m was also somewhat longer. It was of much stronger construction, with greater use of dressed oak uprights, base beams and door sills; at least seven rooms had been floored with timber planking on joists, showing that a much more determined effort had been made to overcome the subsidence created by the Period I ditch below.[33]

The individual components of the new *praetorium* show it to have had nearly 20 rooms in the west wing alone – the remainder, in which bedrooms, dining and reception rooms must have been located, was inaccessible to excavation [34] There were two corridors, one, some 30m long, running north-south, giving access to the six rooms fronting the *via principalis* and dividing them from another row of five rooms fronting the inner courtyard, the other running east-west, on the north side, next to the presumed position of the headquarters building, *principia*. Further, extending on either side of the south-western corner of the building was a yard, enclosed only by a double line of oak palings interwoven with birch, too flimsy to have supported a roof. In the western part it was floored with clean brown clay, overlying turf laid above the remains of the previous period, while on the eastern side part of the inter-vallum road from Period II had been used to provide a cobbled surface packed with clay, above a rubble sandstone base.

The 'carpeting' of the yard, much thicker in the western part, where there was only a clay surface, was found to contain substantial traces of urine and excreta, as well as the *pupae* of stable flies in vast quantities. It is clear that animals were kept here, not least dogs – for hunting (see chapter 7, below) – and perhaps livestock of other kinds. As well as numerous small objects made of bone, metal and wood, footwear, other leather items and pieces of textile, a great many writing tablets were found here. Remains of bonfires show that attempts – fortunately not entirely successful – were made to burn old tablets, as was the case with another, much larger bonfire on the intervallum road between the *praetorium* and the rampart. A particu-larly large number of writing tablets was also recovered from the road surface of the *via principalis* to the west of the yard.[35]

One of the southernmost rooms, 9.5 x 5.5m, fronting the southern part of the yard and separated from the western part by two narrow rooms, which one might describe as ante-rooms, contained nearly 40 writing tablets, several of them letters addressed to Flavius Cerialis. The two ante-rooms had further parts of his corre-spondence, including letters he had drafted, a good many military reports and various accounts. It may be suggested that the prefect had his private office here, and that he either preferred to deal with official papers in the *praetorium* rather than in the *principia* next door, or that he regularly brought paperwork back from the office.

North of these rooms and projecting into the courtyard was a small square structure, each side just under 3m, identifiable as a kitchen. A meat skewer and writing tablets, which include an inventory of kitchen utensils (194), a recipe (208) and one apparently referring to beer-tasting (482), support this view. An almost complete pen was also found, with iron nib and wooden shaft, with a narrow circular hole through its centre, stained with ink at the junction with the nib. This was the cleanest room in the entire building, with no bracken carpeting. Its clay floor, renewed at least six times, incorporated debris from baking ovens, two of which survived near its eastern wall. The kitchen was connected on the west to another small room, measuring just over 4 by nearly 2.5m, about half of which had had a planking floor, on east-west joists, while the other half had been floored by an old timber door, placed flat and mounted on stones, as the base for something like a small water tank.[36]

Of the six rooms fronting the *via principalis* – all of which produced writing tablets – at least one, the largest and most northerly, measuring nearly 6.5 by nearly 5m, was certainly a workshop, with a spread of coal dust, charcoal and ashes over its entire floor and with seven shallow pits. Finds included crucible fragments, a great many metal objects, bronze/copper alloys, pieces of iron and lead and wooden objects – an industrial plane, a lock mechanism and barrel parts – as well as assorted leather items and a few pieces of textile. A smith or armourer had been at work here. Some of the other rooms in this range and in the long corridor on their east and south sides may also have been used by craftsmen, to judge from finds such as wooden wedges, needles, scrapers, bobbins, knives and a drill bit. One room contained a pile of over 100 oak roofing shingles and another had a small rectangular pit, boarded over with old shingles, near the middle of its southern wall.[37]

After being stationed at Vindolanda for little more than a dozen years, the Ninth Batavians were evidently summoned, in summer 105, to reinforce the army on the Danube front for Trajan's Second Dacian War, and never returned to Britain. Their clearing up on the eve of departure seems to have been hasty and messy. Some rooms were left in a filthy state, as was the yard. The armourer left a great many fragments of metal and several utensils in his workshops. Piles of smashed pottery and still functioning wooden shovels, tent pegs and scrapers lay in large quantities in the long corridor. In some parts of the building, the floors were littered with discarded shoes, leather offcuts and dilapidated tentage.[38] The regiment, most of whom had been comfortably housed for years, suddenly had to get ready to camp out every night – except for the crossing over the North Sea – during the long journey which would take them to a fort, Buridava, in what is now Romania. Tiles have been found there datable to precisely this period, stamped CIXB.[39]

45 *An early morning view, after a dry night. The wattle fence is a Period IV room partition*

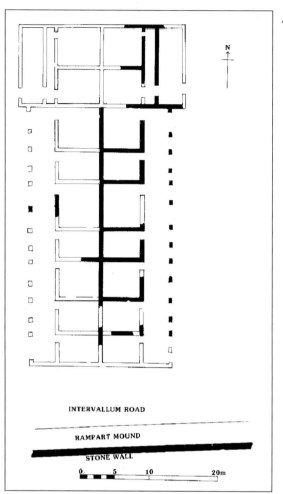

46 *Restored plan of the Period IV barracks. The centurion's quarters are at the north end. The verandas were later blocked in, probably when legionaries arrived*

INTERVALLUM ROAD

RAMPART MOUND

STONE WALL

The return of the Tungrians

There was a gap of several months, well into the autumn, before a replacement garrison arrived. Leaves, mainly birch and oak, had blown into many of the rooms and lay, mixed with birds' feathers and animal excreta, above the bracken carpeting. Squirrels had taken the opportunity to bury hazelnuts in at least seven separate places. Before they could collect these stores, presumably before December 105, the new garrison arrived: it was the First Tungrians again, who were to remain for several decades, perhaps into the 140s. Their demolition gang dismantled the entire *praetorium*. They salvaged the major cross-beams, roof spars and much of the floor planking. The main uprights were cut down some 30cm above floor level and removed. Some of the internal wattle and daub partition walls were ripped out; others, still solidly packed with clay and plastered, were left standing to a height of 1m, leaning over to one side. A heavy wrecking bar found at the foot of one partition wall was probably forgotten by one of the demolition team. Meanwhile the south gate was blocked with dirty turf and clay and a stone wall, 1.2m wide and dressed with clay, was built into the rampart's south face. A new gate must have been constructed further to the west. The intervallum road continued in use, but the old *via principalis* was covered with turf, raising its level to that of the new building, which extended a good 10m further west than the *praetorium* which it replaced. It measured about 46.5m from north to south by at least 20.5m from east to west, and can be identified as a double barrack-block.

Another substantial building, incorporating a massive baking oven, may have been the commanding officer's residence from this period – a further hint to this effect is the predominance among the pottery of decorated samian. A mason's trowel, complete with wooden handle, had pieces of *opus signinum* adhering to the blade. The man who lost it was probably constructing an internal bath-suite close by. But excavation here is still in progress; the building could belong to Period V (cf. below). At all events, it lay well to the west of the Batavians' *praetorium*, and its occupants had the same sort of problem with sinkage caused by the western ditches of the Period I fort that the Batavians experienced. A barrack-block over the site of the demolished Batavians' *praetorium* means that the lay-out of the fort had been altered. It seems likely that the Tungrians' Period IV fort was even larger than that of the Batavians in Periods II-III. If so, the Tungrians, seeing that their unit was 20 per cent smaller in size than the Ninth Batavians, were probably not its only occupants.[40]

The best evidence that the Tungrians were back is a letter (295) to their prefect Priscinus. This period lasted from *c*.105 until about 122. An account (186) naming the consuls of 111 is a firm guide to dating and another Period IV tablet (344) contains at least a strong hint that it was written early in 122 (cf. chapter 6). Much greater use was

47   A wooden clog to wear in the baths

48   TV II 186: the consuls of AD 111 are named in capital letters at the bottom of this sheet

made of oak than in the previous two periods. This allowed analysis by dendrochronology, which showed that some at least of the timbers had been seasoned for a year or two: the felling dates seem to have been 103-4. Among the finds, there was less leatherwork than in the previous two periods and no evidence for metal-working of the kind observed in the Period III *praetorium*. A good many of the rooms produced writing tablets, although far fewer in total than from Period III; in a few cases, tablets from that period had been shifted into the new Period IV building during demolition and construction.[41]

The Tungrians still had no cavalry, even if the prefect and the centurions had their own horses. But a writing tablet from this period (181) shows that a detachment of cavalry from another regiment, the part-mounted First Cohort of Vardulli, a unit first raised in northern Spain, was at Vindolanda. Towards the end of Period IV, building work on Hadrian's Wall was to begin, launched by the Emperor in person on his visit in AD 122 and undertaken by the legions; some legionary soldiers are registered in another tablet from Period IV (180). The arrival of these men may have been the reason for modifications detectable in the buildings of this phase.

A revolt had flared up in Britain on Hadrian's accession (August AD 117),[42] and this surely played a part in his decision to mark the frontier by a continuous wall and other works. The significance of these troubles has sometimes been played down. However, as revealed by a tombstone, reused in a late fourth-century building at Vindolanda, a centurion called T(itus) Ann[ius], serving in the Tungrians, probably as their acting-commander, had been 'killed in the war'. The style of the epitaph fits best a dating in the early second century, and no other war in Britain is known then, apart from the

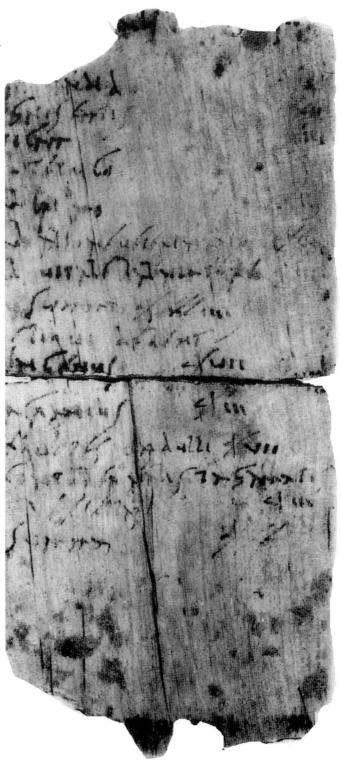

49 TV II 181: the
   Vardullian cavalry
   (equites Vardulli) are
   named in the fourth
   line from the bottom

50   The tombstone of a centurion of the Tungrians, 'T. Ann[ius], killed in the war'

revolt that began in 117.[43] It may be inferred that there was some heavy fighting involving the First Tungrians, although not necessarily in the immediate vicinity, tempting though it might be to think of a 'Battle of Vindolanda' in or soon after AD 117. One of the British peoples who may be assumed to have attacked the Roman garrisons was probably the Anavionenses: it is plausible to infer that conscription of their men some years earlier had left lasting resentment.[44] At all events, more than a set of frontier skirmishes was involved. The legions of the province, perhaps only two at this time, II Augusta and XX Valeria Victrix, also suffered losses. An inscription from Italy shows that 3000 men, drawn from three separate legions, were sent to Britain

51 A typical Period V major post, morticed to take a horizontal beam

under Hadrian: this may give an indication of how many legionaries were killed.[45] The orator Cornelius Fronto, writing 40 years later, stressed the heavy Roman losses under Hadrian 'at the hands of the Britons and of the Jews'.[46]

In Judaea, the revolt led by Bar-Kokhba, which broke out in 132 and lasted for four years, seems to have wiped out a whole legion (XXII Deiotariana).[47] The war in Britain may not have been quite so drastic. Contrary to the traditional view – that it was so seriously damaged by the British rebels that it was disbanded – the Ninth Legion was probably not even stationed in Britain any longer at this time. It seems to have survived Hadrian's reign, to meet its end later, perhaps on the eastern frontier in the early 160s.[48] Even so, the northern part of the province had surely been badly affected. Hadrian's response was to be on a grandiose and hitherto unknown scale: the 'barbarians' were to be 'divided from the Romans' by a continuous stone barrier from sea to sea.[49]

The Emperor arrived in person, in AD 122, probably in June or early July of that year, bringing a new governor, his old friend Aulus Platorius Nepos, and a new legion, VI Victrix, previously stationed on the Lower Rhine at Vetera (Xanten), which would take over the Ninth legion's old base at Eburacum. By then the revolt had been crushed.[50] A fascinating sidelight on the imperial visit is revealed by a writing tablet (344). It is a draft letter of appeal, or protest, from a man who had been severely beaten by the centurions, unjustly as he claimed, addressed to 'Your Majesty'. The writer, evidently a civilian merchant, insists that he should not have been beaten, since he is innocent of any wrong-doing – and anyway, he particularly stresses, he was from 'overseas', *tra(n)smarinus*. By implication, it was perfectly in order to beat native Britons. 'Your Majesty' was surely Hadrian himself, in the area to supervise the start of Wall construction, and awaited at Vindolanda. The unknown complainant had no doubt heard that Hadrian was approachable: a 'man of the people', or *civilis princeps*.[51] Whether the Emperor ever received a fair copy of the indignant letter is another matter.

The draft was found in the centurion's quarters and it may be guessed that it had been confiscated – and that the writer was beaten again.[52]

The site occupied by the barrack-block was levelled at about this time. It was replaced by a building, labelled Period V, of higher quality, with larger rooms, many floored by heavy flags – and its two drains were lined with stone rather than wattle. The western walls of the smaller rooms were constructed of massive oak posts at intervals of 1.75m, set in a trench filled with stone. The posts had mortice holes and insets for horizontal beams, features not found in any earlier buildings at Vindolanda. Wattle walls, bonded with clay, formed the partitions between rooms, but with a double series of posts, of alder and birch, more substantial than those previously used. The finds include far fewer writing tablets than in Periods II-IV but, as well as pottery, there is a good selection of metal objects such as brooches, rings, knives, spatulae, sickles, chisels, and other tools; articles of wood, such as combs, scrapers, spokes, barrel parts; leather items of all kinds, especially shoes, and 11 coins, ranging in date from the time of Vespasian to late in Hadrian's reign, with issues of Trajan predominating. One may note further a lump of coal, pottery, bone and glass counters and beads, whetstones and a door-knocker.

Exactly when the Period IV barrack was demolished and replaced is not clear. At all events, north of it was erected at the start of Period V another building more elaborate and expensive than anything previously constructed at Vindolanda. Its erection may well have followed instructions from the governor, as soon as he was informed that Hadrian was on his way to Britain and wished to deal with the 'frontier question' in person. The Emperor had to be found quarters in the area, and Vindolanda was ideally placed as a base from which to inspect the central sector of his new planned Wall. (Several other forts doubtless had to undertake similar preparations.) Massive oak posts were used, the flooring was of *opus signinum* and most of the internal walls were finished with plaster, some of it painted. Only the western part of what was no doubt a large courtyard building could be examined. The quality of finds from this part of the site suggests that its occupants were of higher status than those stationed at Vindolanda in Periods I-IV.[53] It is worth asking whether the governor Platorius Nepos was later housed here. He would have needed accommodation, since it must be assumed that he spent a good deal of time on the spot over the next few years, to direct the progress of Wall-building. The building further to the west discovered in 2001, from Period IV or V, may indeed be another part of what would then have been a very large complex.

The Tungrians remained at Vindolanda for some years after the Wall was built, and were responsible for Period V: a complete spearhead found in the packing above a Period V floor has a punched inscription on the blade, TVNG,[54] and a diploma issued in 146 to a veteran of the regiment, recruited in 121, was found in the later stone fort.[55] Eventually they were to be based at nearby Housesteads. Which regiment replaced them at Vindolanda is not certain, perhaps the Second or the Third Cohort of Nervians. Likewise not yet clear is the relationship of the Period V buildings to the first stone fort at Vindolanda. At any rate, the unit stationed here from the third to the early fifth century was a different one, the Fourth Cohort of Gauls.[56]

5 Military routine

The strength report of the First Tungrians

The earliest writing tablet is a strength report of the First Tungrians (154), from the filled-in inner western ditch of the first fort. It is not known whether the compiling of such reports was a routine feature of the prefect's duties – nor why this one ended up in the ditch. Presumably a fair copy had been sent to provincial or district headquarters. The document is exceptional, of oak rather than birch or alder, and twice the size of the usual leaf tablets. It lists the disposition of the unit on 18 May in an unnamed year, under the prefect Julius Verecundus: 456 men were absent, including five centurions, with only 296, one a centurion, present. Of the absentees, 337 men and two centurions were at Coria (Corbridge), 20km east along the Stanegate, and 46 were serving as 'guards, *singulares*, of the legate, on the staff, *officio*, of Ferox'. The 337 at Coria may have been new recruits (as suggested in the previous chapter).

Ferox was not previously known and cannot be positively identified. Since later tablets regularly refer to the governor as the *consularis* not legate, he is most likely to have been legate of a legion. But he could have been acting-governor as well, indeed should have been, to have guards not drawn from his own legion. After Agricola's departure early in 84, only one governor is known during the next decade, by a single sentence in Suetonius (*Dom.* 10.3). He claims that Domitian 'put Sallustius Lucullus the governor of Britain to death because he allowed a new type of lance to be named *Lucullean*'. This was presumably construed as treason. At any rate, the sudden downfall of a governor could have led to a legionary legate (or the *iuridicus*) being appointed as temporary replacement.[1] There are various possible occasions with which the execution of Lucullus might be connected: Domitian had to suppress several conspiracies before the one that led to his murder in September 96. Sacrifices were made at Rome on 22 September 87 'because of the detection of the crimes of nefarious men'. This was the same year as the abandonment of the Inchtuthil fortress and other bases beyond the Forth, the inevitable consequence of removing from Britain II Adiutrix and several auxiliary regiments. Had Lucullus objected? Another possibility is in or soon after January 89, when the governor of Upper Germany, Antonius Saturninus, attempted a coup d'état. He was soon suppressed, and his colleague in Britain might have been accused of involvement. A third conceivable moment for Lucullus' death is the period after late summer 93. According to Tacitus, the 'terror', in which 'so many men of consular rank were slaughtered', began after Agricola's death on 23 August that year (*Agr.* 44-5).[2]

52 *TV II 154: the strength report of the First Tungrians, found in the innermost Period I ditch*

On the other hand, the limited evidence for Vindolanda's Period I suggests that late 93 is too late for Ferox to have been acting governor *if* he served after Lucullus' death – all this is of course very hypothetical. At any rate, a probable consequence of the governor's downfall is revealed by other evidence. An auxiliary unit with a surprising name, *pedites singulares Britannici*, 'infantry guardsmen from Britain', i.e. ex-guards of the governor of Britain, is found in the army of the Danubian province Upper Moesia in 103. The removal of the British governor's personal guards to another province is best explained in connection with the Lucullus affair.[3] The fairly rare name Ferox is attested for only by two senators. Both, as it happens, could have commanded a legion under Domitian: Cn. Pompeius Ferox Licinianus (consul in 98) and Ti. Julius Ferox (consul 99). Julius Ferox, a correspondent of the Younger Pliny, who shared his literary activities (*Epp.* 7.13), is likelier on present evidence to be the legate in the strength report: Pliny refers to him *c.*AD 112 as a former governor of a military province (10.87.3).[4]

To return after this digression to the Tungrians at Vindolanda: the other absentees were one centurion at Londinium; six soldiers and one centurion at another place, name illegible, as is the purpose of their mission; nine in Gaul, *in Gallia*, with one centurion, probably collecting supplies, e.g. clothing, and 11 who had gone to collect the unit's pay, *stipendiatum*, perhaps at Eburacum (York).[5] Distribution of pay (*numeratio*) is mentioned in a Period III letter (242) and one from Period IV (327) refers to men carrying coins, specified as 'in small change', *in aere minuto*. Of the 296, including one centurion, who remained at Vindolanda, 31 were registered as unfit for duty: 15 'ill', *aegri*, six 'wounded', *volnerati*, and ten 'with eye-inflammation', *lippientes*. It might seem tempting to think that the wounded were casualties of Mons Graupius. But even if the report belonged to 84, the year after the battle, would men wounded in September 83 still be out of action in mid-May the next year? The six could have been wounded in a minor skirmish – or injured in the course of normal military training or building work. Sufferers from eye-disease, *lippitudo*, were a common sight in ancient Rome. *Lippientes* were unfit for work but not necessarily confined to bed. They could hang about all day and were bracketed by the poet Horace with barbers as typical purveyors of gossip (*Satires* 1.7.3). *Lippitudo* was a description covering various minor eye-troubles. Apart from avoidance of direct light, the standard treatment was by a salve or ointment. Hundreds of oculists' stamps are known, mainly in the north-western part of the empire, used to impress on the block of ointment, *collyrium*, the maker's name and the contents of his remedy. At least seven oculists whose stamps have been found in Britain produced salves to treat *lippitudo*, with ingredients such as poppy or celandine and myrrh 'to be used twice a day with egg'.[6]

It is unfortunate that the strength report supplies no names, other than those of the prefect and the legate. Slight compensation is provided by part of a list of soldiers, also found in the Period I ditch (161), on which the names Fuscus, Settius, Expeditus, Albinus, Verecund[us], Celer(?) and Festus are legible. All are Latin, except for the Celtic Settius. A stylus tablet from Period I (Inv. 836) names Montanus *sig(nifer)*, standard-bearer, and another (Inv. 787) contains welcome confirmation that the Tungrians were the garrison, *c(o)ho(rtis) Tung(rorum)* in the address.

The *renuntia* of the Ninth Batavians

Vindolanda has produced nearly three dozen examples of another kind of 'report', called *renuntium*. It referred to an inspection by the senior NCOs of the Ninth Batavians, one of whom delivered it, clearly to the prefect. No documents quite like this are known elsewhere in the Empire. But it could easily have been standard army practice to write them. Where the name of the unit is sufficiently preserved, in full or part, it is that of the Ninth Cohort of Batavians, and it may be assumed that all derive from this unit. Virtually all come from Period III, probably during the term of office of Flavius Cerialis, and most of them from the enclosed yard (Room VIA) outside the three southernmost rooms in the west wing of his *praetorium*. All but one (1418) are fragments. It can be guessed that the prefect tore the old one up, as soon as a new one was handed in – and perhaps he threw the pieces out of the window. More likely is that the majority were intended to be burned, with other 'waste paper', when the Batavians were evacuating the fort.

The *renuntia* have a standard formula. At the top comes the date, with day and month (but not the year), and 'report of the Ninth Cohort of Batavians', *renuntium cohortis VIIII Batavorum*. Then comes the laconic text, in Latin a mere seven words: *omnes ad loca* (or *locum*) *qui debunt et impedimenta*, 'All at their places [or place] who ought to be, and the equipment (is intact)'. In the nine examples where it survives the spelling *debunt* is a variation for the standard Latin *debent*.[7] The text regularly concludes with the statement that 'the *optiones* and *curatores* reported: A, *optio* of the century of B, delivered (the report)'. The *optiones* were the deputy-centurions; it is not quite certain who the *curatores* were. The word can just mean 'overseer' and perhaps was applied to the NCOs in charge of equipment. Alternatively it might be a title for deputy-decurions. The names of the *optiones* Verecundus, Arquittius, Justinus and Candidus are preserved as the men who delivered the *renuntium*. Of the centurions, we have the names of Crescens, Exomnius, Felicio and Rufus.

Seven examples have 'places', four 'place', in the rest the word is missing: it is unclear whether the variation had a real meaning and whether the word just means 'at their post'. But it is worth remarking that small detachments of the cohort are known to have been stationed out, probably on a regular basis. A letter from the decurion Masclus (his name, also written 'Masculus', means 'male') to Cerialis (1544) begins by asking 'whether we should all return with the *vexillum*?'.[8] Temporary detachments, whether from legions or auxiliary regiments, were regularly assigned a *vexillum*, flag. Perhaps Masclus' outpost, and others like it, were known as *loca*. But it seems likelier that the *renuntia* were reports on all the men in the regiment and all the equipment.

Masclus' letter was doubtless brought to Vindolanda from the outstation by one of his troopers. At the opening of the letter he actually addresses the prefect as 'Cerialis, his king', a form of extreme flattery often applied by poets to their patrons – although the possibility that Cerialis, like the earlier prefect of Batavians Julius Civilis, was indeed 'of royal stock' should not be ruled out.[9] Masclus ends his letter with the wish that Cerialis 'may be very happy and propitious to me',

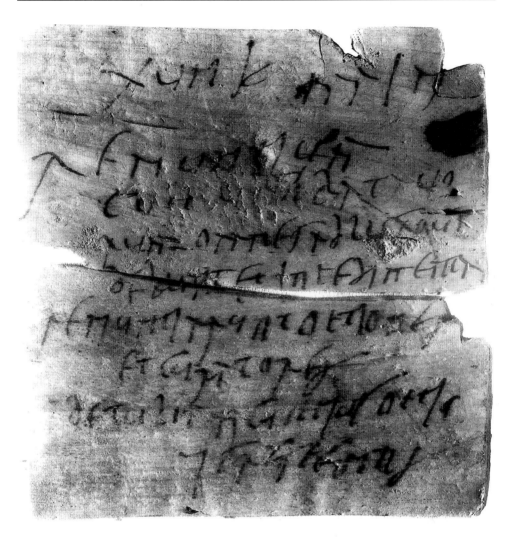

53   The only complete renuntium: Inv. 1418

and, by way of a PS, adds what one suspects was his real reason for writing: 'the comrades have no beer, which I ask that you order to be sent.' Noticeable also is the oddity that Masclus writes the word 'have' *habunt* instead of the normal *habent*, the same variant as *debunt* for *debent* in the *renuntia*. Another, fragmentary letter (505) from this decurion (in the address he spells his name Masculus), clearly also to his prefect (part of the closing greeting, *[domi]ne bene valere*, survives) was found in a period II level, which perhaps suggests that he was stationed out for some time. A letter (242) from Cerialis to Felicio, one of his centurions, written in early September (also found in the yard outside the *praetorium*), suggests that Felicio was in charge of an outstationed detachment, in this case fairly close to the fort, and brought Cerialis' letter back with him.

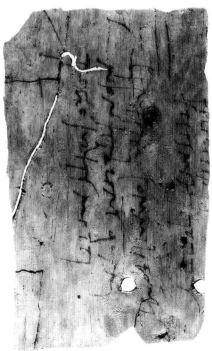

54   The letter from the decurion Masclus (Inv. 1544); for the address see. **33**

   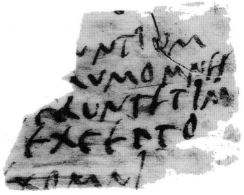

55   The letter from Cerialis to Felicio (242)   *56   Someone not at his place (Inv. 1482)*

'Tomorrow, early in the morning, come to Vindolanda to [take part in?] the payment of the century.' A second man who was apparently a centurion, [Cl]odius Super, wrote to Cerialis (255) asking that a number of woollen cloaks and tunics be sent him, 'which I need for the use of my boys'. The 'boys' could mean his slaves, but it might refer to the soldiers in his detachment.

Only on one *renuntium* is an exception registered: 'all at their posts who should be except for' a man whose name is missing 'from the century of Exomnius' (1482). Was he just absent without leave – or had he deserted? A fragmentary draft letter by Cerialis (226) refers to deserters and the same word recurs in a fragmentary letter sent to Vindolanda at this time (320). Something of this sort may also be referred to in a letter which one of Cerialis' predecessors, in Period II, received from a colleague, Celonius Justus (345). Justus writes of sending men back (presumably to Vindolanda) in the charge of the decurion Atto, and adds, 'I ask you, brother, to strike them off the list at once.' Another, rather dramatic, episode is hinted at in a fragment (1340), from a letter presumably addressed to a Vindolanda garrison commander: ' . . . of those involved in the case he has been ordered to transport one man from the province in chains'.

A further fragment (Inv. 953) perhaps refers to something similar, if relatively low-key: 'I ask that you receive . . . , so that . . . him, fettered, through . . . ', *rogo adsumes ut eum constrictum per... .*[10] The man who was to be deported from Britain must have committed a serious crime. Several cases of desertion may have been motivated by the simple wish to evade further military service – or to remain in the Vindolanda area, where several men had probably found local girlfriends, if rumours spread that the Batavians were going to move to the Danube lands.

The date is preserved more or less complete on only eight *renuntia*: 18 or 28 January, 14 February, between 8 and 13 March, 8 April, 15 April, 22 June, 6 July and 24 December. It is impossible to make out any pattern from these dates, and

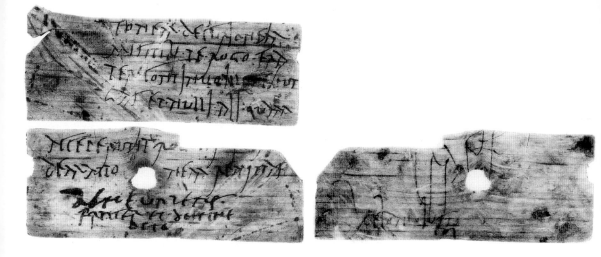

57   Celonius Justus asks his colleague to 'strike them off the list' (345)

58   A man is to be deported from the province in chains (vinculis: Inv. 1340)

59   Messicus asks to spend his leave at Coria (175)

it is no doubt pure coincidence that the months from August to November are not represented. The only complete example (1418), that from 15 April, a *renuntium* delivered by Arquittius, *optio* in the century of Crescens, was found with the pile of tablets and other 'rubbish' outside the *praetorium*, close to the south gate, where they had been set on fire. It was Arquittius who handed in the report dated 8 April. Of course, this need not have been just seven days before his other report – it might have been in a different year. But there is at least a slight chance that reports were made every seven days.

Applications for leave

Twelve fragmentary tablets, all torn up, like almost all the *renuntia*, presumably when no longer relevant, and also mostly found in the yard outside the *praetorium*, are short letters with a more or less identical text, requesting permission to go on leave. Six are specifically to 'Lord Cerialis', one is to 'Lord Flavianus', a predecessor of Cerialis' in Period II, probably Hostilius Flavianus (172, cf. 261), and one is to Priscinus (173), prefect of the First Cohort of Tungrians in period IV (295-8). The prefect's name in the other four is not preserved, but it was probably that of Cerialis. The soldier begins with his name and century – or in one case probably his squadron (*turma*) – and continues: 'I ask you, Lord Cerialis, that you hold me worthy for you to grant me leave'. In three cases the applications state the place where the leave is to be spent – at Coria (Corbridge) in two (175, 176); at Ulucium, a not yet identified fort, perhaps at Newbrough, between Vindolanda and Coria, where the Third Cohort of Batavians may have been stationed (cf. 311), in the other (174).[11] In one (176) the applicant, Buccus, adds the reason why he wants leave at Coria: 'so that I can buy (?)' something, perhaps for his 'relatives' (*fam[iliaribus]*?). One applicant (177) asks the CO to write to another prefect, presumably the man commanding the other fort.

It is worth remarking that at other periods the right to go on leave was far from being recognised. Soldiers could not get it unless they paid a 'fee' to a centurion.[12] To judge from these Vindolanda applications, although the soldiers were careful to phrase the request with extreme courtesy, there seems no question but that it was normally granted – and it is hard to believe that Cerialis made the applicants pay a fee.

Official correspondence

A little insight into the way the frontier district was being run is given in a letter to Flavius Cerialis from his brother-officer Claudius Karus (250; cf. 251 for Karus' full name): 'Brigionus has asked me, Lord, to recommend him to you. I ask therefore, Lord, whether you would be willing to support him in what he asks of you. I ask you that you may be willing to recommend him to Annius Equester, regional centurion, at

Luguvalium.' It is not known exactly what were the duties or powers of a 'regional centurion', *centurio regionarius*. This letter suggests that Equester, who was surely seconded from a legion rather than an auxiliary centurion, was based at Luguvalium. It is plausible that he acted as a kind of district officer, keeping the native population under control. Some division of responsibility must have been involved at Luguvalium. The garrison there included a cavalry unit, or had done so at any rate not many years before, the *ala Sebosiana*.[13] A prefect of cavalry would have outranked a legionary centurion. On the other hand, the latter was probably directly responsible to his legate, no doubt of the Ninth Legion at Eburacum. One can only guess what Brigionus was hoping for from Equester. He might have been a travelling salesman for all we know. A name beginning Brig- looks Celtic, but it is not otherwise attested. He could have been a native Briton. Perhaps he was hoping to be employed as an interpreter. Coincidence or not, a fragmentary tablet also from Period III (188), probably an account, has a name beginning Brigio (the rest illegible or missing). Perhaps Brigionus ended up by staying at Vindolanda and being given some appointment by Cerialis.

Several letters are preserved from decurions of a cavalry regiment or a part-mounted cohort, although the *ala Sebosiana* is not yet attested in the Vindolanda tablets. A fragmentary letter (284), to one of the prefects of the Ninth from a decurion called [Cla]udius (?) Verus, is too scrappy to deliver any connected sense. On another tablet (1353), of which only part of the address survives, the name of the writer, Veri[anus] and his rank, dec(urion) of the *ala Petriana*, can be read. Another man from the *ala Petriana*, then stationed at Coria, again probably a decurion, called Cluvius Florus, wrote (281) to someone in the Ninth Batavians, probably the prefect, mentioning 'a petition (?), which I myself will bring to you'. Cluvius Florus is also attested by the opening of a letter from him to a man called Quintus (1361) – the rest of the tablet looks blank, but has perhaps been washed clean.[14]

The commanding officers of these auxiliary regiments clearly had to deal with petitions of all sorts and to act as judges. A letter (322) found in the Period III *praetorium* looks very much like such an appeal for action to the prefect. What survives refers to 'slaves', *servorum*, and ends with the words 'and they filched my (military) belt', *balteus*, possibly while the writer was at the baths, if the word ending *-neo* that comes before *servorum* may be restored as *[bal]neo*. No doubt the writer had named those whom he regarded as the thieves. For comparison, one may note the letter from the *corniularius* Ascanius (1187), complaining about a man, presumably in another unit, who had not repaid him a considerable sum of money, perhaps as much as 250 *denarii*. Ascanius apparently writes: 'I assign that to the cognisance of his prefect', *assigno id ad conscientiam praefecti sui*.[15]

A fragmentary draft (317), perhaps in Cerialis' handwriting, of a letter intended to be sent to a man in higher authority, seems to show him involved with a forthcoming trial: near the beginning come the words 'as you ordered', followed two lines later by *cognitionem*, 'legal investigation'. Another, even more fragmentary draft by Cerialis (238) also looks like a 'business' letter. The first words are: 'if, to my concern, Lord', *si sollicitudini meae domin[e]*. But he did not write much more – after '[the matter?] has been settled', *explicata est*, in the next line, he seems to have crossed the whole line out and laid the tablet aside. Much more complete – most of the second page survives – and

60 Ascanius complains about an unpaid debt (Inv. 1187)

informative is a letter to Cerialis from a decurion called Vitalis (263). He refers to 'my letter, which you received from Equester, centurion of the Third Cohort of Batavians, [which I sent(?)] to you on 30 April.' Vitalis ends by greeting 'my Lady', *dominam*, surely Cerialis' wife Lepidina. This suggests that he had previously been a visitor at Vindolanda. On this occasion Equester, perhaps returning from Luguvalium to the Third Batavians' fort – at Ulucium? – somewhere to the east of Vindolanda, perhaps at Newbrough between Vindolanda and Coria, had served as courier.

Coria and Luguvalium, the two major military bases to east and west of Vindolanda, probably generated most of the outside activity for the Vindolanda officers. A single sentence in a letter to Cerialis (266) contains the request: 'I want him to come to me at Coria and receive . . . ' The writer was no doubt either the commander of the Coria garrison, the *ala Petriana*, or some visiting higher officer. The reverse procedure – men being sent to Vindolanda – is illustrated by a fragmentary letter from Cerialis' colleague Caecilius September (252), in which only the concluding sentence is preserved: 'I have sent you . . . by a cavalryman. Farewell, Lord brother.' The same phrase evidently occurs in another fragment from a letter to Cerialis (268), and another Period III letter (318), probably also to Cerialis, has the sentence: 'my Lord, I have sent you . . . from the cohort which I command, so that you can . . . '. A fragmentary Period IV letter (1409) contains the phrase 'I have sent . . . back to the fort (*dimisi ad castra*)', followed by 'I want you to know that, except for one cavalryman, I . . . for two days'. Yet another fragmentary letter (1518) preserves the following from the first page: 'I have instructed [ ], so that certain things which I think relate to your office, *officium* (or: to your official position) . . . ' On the back the writer concludes: 'I ask that you, my Lord, let me know what you think about this business.'

Much better preserved are two letters to Vindolanda prefects, in each case concerning the Commander-in-Chief, 'our Consular', as they called the governor of Britain. The first, to Cerialis (248), was written jointly by two colleagues:

> Niger and Brocchus greet their Cerialis.
> We wish, brother, that what you are about to do will be most successful.
> It will, indeed, be so, both because it accords with our wishes to make this prayer for you and because you thoroughly deserve it. You will certainly meet our Consular quite soon.
> [then, in a different handwriting, comes the closing greeting]
> We wish, brother, that you are in good health, Lord.

After this two more words were added, perhaps 'expect us'.
Priscinus received a letter (295) from another colleague named Niger, possibly not the same Niger as the man who wrote the previous letter:

> Oppius Niger greets his Priscinus.
> Crispus and Te[rtius?] from the First Cohort of Tungrians, whom you sent with a letter to our Consular, [I have sent on] from Bremetennacum (Ribchester) to Lindum (?) (Lincoln) . . . on 1 February.
> Farewell, Lord brother.

61 Niger and Brocchus write to Cerialis (248)

Travelling expenses

The two soldiers from the First Tungrians will have been given travelling-money for this mission, which was to take them halfway across the province. An even longer journey is revealed in a letter probably sent to Cerialis (283: the name in the address is very faint). It refers to being on the way to Rome (*Romam petere*), travelling-expenses, *viaticum*, and *tabulas*, probably writing tablets. Travelling money is also mentioned in another Period III letter (330), in this case by the applicant himself (*viatico meó*). An account (185) from Period II shows travelling expenses for July, which could have been incurred by a soldier on official business, in this case probably going to the legionary base at Eburacum via Coria. It evidently concerned a journey from Vindolanda and back again: Vinovia (Binchester), Cataractonium (Catterick) and Isurium (Aldborough), all on the Roman 'Great North Road', are named as stopping-places. The legible part of the incomplete tablet notes a small sum, 0.25 *denarius*, paid out for *faex*, 'wine-lees', a cheap form of refreshment, at Isurium, then, perhaps at Eburacum, more wine-lees, and barley – presumably for the mules. A repair to the vehicle was then necessary – two axles for the wagon, at a cost of 3.5 *denarii*, are registered. Then, evidently on the return journey, come wine-lees for 0.25 *denarius* at Isurium once more, and the same again at Cataractonium, where 0.5 *denarius* was also paid out for a *locarium*, a lodging, the final payments being at Vinovia, including a small sum for wheat. Total costs were listed as 'making 78.75 *denarii*, grand total 94.75 *denarii*.' Isurium crops up again in a very fragmentary account (1405) from Period III or IV: 'daily, . . . March, at Isurium', followed by '8 *sextarii*'. A *sextarius* was a liquid measure equivalent to about half a litre or a pint.

Working parties

Two fragmentary documents of another kind from Period III show groups of soldiers from the Ninth Batavians at work at Vindolanda itself. On 7 March (156) 30 *structores*, 'builders', were sent to 'make the guest-house', *ad hospiti[u]m . . . faciendum*. They were accompanied by the *medicus* Marcus, evidently a standard precaution with Roman military work-detachments, in case any of the men sustained injury. Others were assigned to 'burning stone', presumably quarried nearby and burned to produce lime for mortar, and a third party was preparing clay for 'the fort's wattle-fences'. The other tablet (155), dated 25 April, has more detail: 343 men in all were 'in the workshops'. Of these, 12 were leather-workers or shoemakers, *sutores*, and 18 were builders, *structores*, at the bath-house. Others — the numbers are missing — were working lead, *plumbum*, used not least for water-pipes; at work on a hospital, *valetudinarium*; 'at the kilns', no doubt, firing tiles and bricks; digging clay; plastering; making tents; and preparing rubble. The bath-house that was under construction has been located on the south side of the fort, an elaborate structure of stone, with the standard hypocaust pillars and flues made of tile. An even more fragmentary tablet (160) from Period V, when the First Tungrians were in garrison again, evidently listed a whole series of individuals, giving the name of each man's centurion; and, in a few cases, a term describing their function can be read: four were labelled *faber*, carpenter, and one was probably a shield-maker, *[sc]utarius*.

62   Travelling expenses (185)

Supply

One of the tasks for outstationed detachments was no doubt concerned with supply. The decurion Masclus, whose detachment was not far from Vindolanda, is recorded on a grain account (1495). Among 'receipts' early in June is registered 'from Masclus *dec.*, wheat (*siligo*)'; a few days later more wheat was received from Vitalis (rank unspecified) and in early September came another delivery by Masclus. Masclus and his men perhaps had the task of escorting grain-wagons. In an almost complete letter from a Period II level (1108: the ink is very faded), the writer tells his correspondent that 'you will receive out of the Britons' wagons . . . from Ricarromaucus, 381 *modii* of *bracis*'. *Bracis* was a cereal of uncertain type used for making beer; a *modius*

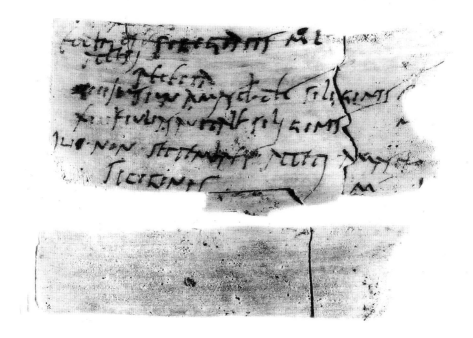

63   Masclus delivers wheat (Inv. 1495)

contained some 8.75 litres dry measure and the Britons had evidently loaded 53 *modii* per wagon. The grain was apparently reloaded onto slightly larger wagons, holding 63 *modii* each. In the second half of the letter transport costs are discussed, and the writer comments, 'if you provide Verecundus with grain for his men'. This might be Julius Verecundus, prefect of the First Tungrians in Period I (in which case the tablet may have 'moved' into a higher level when the Period II fort was built).

Two letters to a man called Cassius Saecularis, who, as a Roman citizen, must surely have been at least a centurion – unless he was a civilian trader – show him dealing with supplies, of barley and timber. Part of the second sheet of a letter to him from Curtius Super (213), found in a Period II level, contains the sentence: 'so that you may explain and so that they may get barley from you as commercial goods'. Another correspondent, a *cornic(u)larius*, senior NCO, whose name is not preserved, wrote, in a letter from a Period IV level (215), that 'they will have the authority of Severinus – for I have received it from him – if anyone wants to come, and he will not mind where they are storing the firewood and timber.' Exactly when Saecularis was at Vindolanda is not clear, as the two letters were found in levels separated by a good 15 years: probably that in the Period IV level had been displaced from Period II during construction work. A third letter to the same man (214), from a Period II level, points to him being in the army: only the opening is preserved, but this is unusually informative: 'Vettius [or Vittius] Adiutor, eagle-bearer (*aquilifer*) of legion II Aug(usta), to Cassius Saecularis, his little brother, very many greetings'. One can

64   An eagle-bearer of the Second Legion writes to Vindolanda (214)

only speculate how the two men knew each other so well that a senior NCO of the Second Augusta, stationed far to the south at Isca, could call Saecularis *fraterclus*, 'little brother'.[16] A final, fragmentary tablet (216), with no names preserved, in the same handwriting as Adiutor's letter, and again from a Period II level, contains a phrase probably meaning 'I bought as much as I could'.

A letter from either Period III or IV (1578), to a man called Gabinius Crescens (?), also concerns surplus timber, in this case roofing-shingles. The first sheet is largely illegible. In the second the writer, whose name was perhaps Fidelis, makes an offer: 'I shall gladly produce the 100 shingles which I have at Romanius'. If you do not need them, transport them as an extra when your wagons are coming anyway, and guard them well with your boys so that they do not get trampled on at all.' He ends with greetings for three persons, two of whom are certainly female, one called Ingenua, the other perhaps Varranilla (?).

Food was the most important single item for supply. Olive oil, a major feature of the Roman diet, is so far certainly attested in only one of the writing tablets (203), by contrast with the frequent mention of wine, beer and a whole variety of spices, herbs, meat and cereals. However, finds of amphorae from southern Spain, several datable to the period of the writing tablets, show that the Batavians, Tungrians and other soldiers were catered for in this respect as well.[17] The most important item was grain. In Period IV, a man called Octavius was dealing in unthreshed grain, 'ears of corn', *spicas*, on a large scale (343). He tells his correspondent Candidus that he had made a down payment of 300 *denarii* for 5000 *modii*; meanwhile he had threshed 119 *modii* of *bracis*. Sale of barley is referred to in the letter to Saecularis (213), and an account from July in an unknown year registers the unloading of this cereal (1474IV, 1478). A detailed document (180) found close to Octavius' letter – in the centurion's quarters of the Period IV barrack-block – registers the distribution of wheat to individuals and groups of men.

Octavius also refers to having 'completed', presumably treated, 170 hides and to his awaiting another consignment from Cataractonium (Catterick). This major base is known from excavations to have had extensive leather-workshops at this time. Hides were needed for a great range of leather goods, not least tents, saddles, straps and footwear. For tents supple calf leather was required. Delivery of even finer quality

65 *Amphora with
a painted
inscription: the
firm's name,
the Aemilii
and Cassii*

leather is reported in another letter (309), found in the Period III *praetorium* yard: a man called Metto tells his correspondent Advectus that 'I have sent you goatskins, six in number'. This comes at the end of a long list of wooden items, mostly parts for wagons, 'sent through Saco', including '34 wheel-hubs; 38 cart-axles, one of them turned on a lathe; 300 spokes.' To a large extent, leather was worked on site, by the regiment's own cobblers, *sutores* (155).[18]

Wagons crop up in several other tablets. It was probably Flavius Cerialis who was told in a letter that steps had been taken 'that wagons may be given to you' (315) and was advised in another (316) that 'you should weigh up in your mind, my Lord, what quantity of wagons you are going to send to carry stone'. Stone was surely already being quarried just to the north-east of the fort (and perhaps on nearby Barcombe, where it was extensively worked at latest in Hadrian's reign). It may be inferred that the Vindolanda garrison was being required to contribute to a major programme involving several units, most likely road-construction. The surviving part of another Period III letter (314) refers to someone being 'sent to get the lime which you have provided for us. I ask that [the mules?] be loaded straightaway, so that [they can set off?] at first light.' Wagons, mainly drawn by oxen, no doubt played a crucial part in supplying the units in the far north of the province, even if much could be sent by sea and then by boat up the Tyne at least as far as Coria (Corbridge). It is no surprise to find 'oxherds' (*bubulcari*) registered on the Period IV wheat account (180): the eight *modii* assigned to them were sent 'to the wood', probably on the south side of the Chineley burn. The oxherds presumably had their quarters there, while the oxen would be grazing in adjacent meadows.

66   'Consider how many wagons you are going to send' (315)

A good deal had to be sent from a distance, including clothing from Gaul, and miscellaneous items from London. But the Batavians had poultry in a poultry-yard, probably established by the prefect and possibly run at a profit (1474), and both they and the Tungrians in Period IV had a regimental piggery, of which Candidus was in charge for the Batavians and Lucco for the Tungrians (183, 180). 'Piggery' is probably a misleading term: the pigs probably ranged free, supervised by their soldier swineherd, rather than being kept in sties. The Batavians evidently produced their own beer, with a regimental brewer, Atrectus the *cervesarius* (182). Their CO Cerialis was supplied with beer (190) as well as his men (1474A, 1544). The Tungrians consumed large quantities at a remarkably low price (186).

Training and British conscripts

Not a single tablet from Vindolanda refers directly to any fighting. The 'six wounded' men in the First Tungrians' strength report (154) might, but need not, have been in a battle. This may be a little surprising for the reader of the *Agricola*, remembering how at Mons Graupius the great man 'ordered the four Batavian and two Tungrian cohorts to fight hand to hand at sword's point. This was what they had been trained for in their long service, whereas it was awkward for the enemy with their small shields and enormous swords . . . So the Batavians rained blows indiscriminately, struck with their shield-bosses and stabbed in the face' (*Agr.* 36). Some of the men who served at Vindolanda – a good many of the Tungrians in Period I and a fair number of the Batavians in Periods II and III – must have fought at Mons Graupius. But it may well be that no serious military exchanges between Roman forces and Britons had taken place since then. Still, patrols, manoeuvres, parades, weapon training – all these were surely going on during the period of the writing tablets, even if they are not mentioned in the tablets. Patrolling was later a speciality of the Ninth Batavians: the regiment carried the additional title *exploratorum*, the 'scouts'.[19] Perhaps Masclus and his *vexillum* were regularly on patrol. As for training, a fair number of weapons have been found from the time of the Tungrians and Batavians: heads of spears, lances, javelins, arrowheads, possibly artillery bolts (or a different type of arrowhead).[20] The words for these weapons have not yet cropped up in the tablets, apart from a document from Period V (160) which may mention swords (*gladi.[ ]*), and another, rather unusual text. Only six lines survive from a 'memorandum' (164), which deals, not with weapon training by the Vindolanda garrison, but with the Britons' capacity with weapons: ' . . . the Brittones, rather many of them cavalrymen, are naked [perhaps meaning 'without body-armour']. The cavalrymen do not use swords, nor do the *Brittunculi* mount to throw javelins'. *Brittunculi*, a word not previously recorded, is a – literally – belittling name. One can compare the anti-immigrant comment by a contemporary poet. Juvenal raged at the *Graeculus esuriens*, 'the little Greeks on the make' (*Satires* 3.78), who had swamped Rome at the expense of the 'real' Romans. *Brittunculi* may be rendered 'little Brits' – but with an undertone suggesting that 'nasty' or 'pathetic little Brits' was how the writer regarded them. Rather than a description of how an enemy force had performed in a recent battle, it is more likely that it is about how a group of British conscripts were shaping up in training. Several regiments had already been raised in Britain during the previous decades.[21] Only a year or two before this writing tablet, Tacitus commented that 'the Britons submit readily to conscription' (*Agr.* 12.1), and the speech he gives to the Caledonian leader Calgacus before the battle of Mons Graupius treats it as shameful that fellow-Britons are serving in Agricola's army.

The 'memorandum' could either be the rough copy of a report by a Vindolanda prefect, or a letter to a prefect describing the Britons' capacities. If the latter view is correct, it could be that it was an advance briefing for the garrison commander. Other evidence throws more light on these *Brittunculi*. An inscription from Italy gives the long career of a man called Titus Haterius Nepos, who rose to be Prefect of Egypt in 120. He began with service in the equestrian 'three militias'. The units in which he served are not named, but after the third post, as prefect of cavalry, or, more probably, in conjunction with it, Nepos was 'census-officer', *censitor*, of the *Brittones Anavion[enses]* – in other words, of the Britons in Annandale. Heads were surely not counted in such a region to assess liability for monetary tribute – the Anavionenses would not have used money – but to pick out young men suitable for military service. A fragment of a letter from Period II (304) refers to the 'administration of the census', which could well be that conducted by Haterius Nepos. Better still, there is a letter (1379) from Haterius to Flavius Genialis, probably immediate predecessor of Flavius Cerialis as prefect of the Ninth Batavians, *c*.100. Haterius was expecting Genialis to come to Coria (Corbridge); he was surely prefect of the *ala Petriana*, stationed there at this time. Another man, Pro[culus], no doubt also a regimental commander, had received a similar letter, Haterius writes. This was probably Flavius Proculus, a correspondent and brother-officer of Genialis (1337). He could have been the prefect of the Third Batavians at this time.

67   *The inadequacies of the Brittunculi (the first word in the second
bottom line of 164)*

It cannot be coincidence that the *Anavion[enses]* crop up in a fragmentary list on another Vindolanda tablet, which also includes the name Genialis (1475). It seems legit-imate to infer that these were the *Brittunculi*, sent to Vindolanda to be licked into shape. Flavius Genialis could well be the recipient of the derogatory remarks about them: the 'memorandum' may have been prepared by Haterius Nepos, with copies for other prefects to whom batches of conscripts were sent. As for what happened to the *Brittunculi*, or Anavionenses, it seems that the small units of Britons, *numeri Brittonum*, attested on the Roman frontier in Germany by inscriptions from the 140s onwards, had already arrived there about 100. The Anavionenses were probably among them.[22]

The departure of the Batavians, the Third as well as the Ninth, from Britain for the Continent in 105, was followed by some radical retrenching in this northern frontier zone. Garrisons were withdrawn from forts in southern Scotland, including all those in

1   *Aerial view of Vindolanda from the north-west*

2   Aerial view of Vindolanda from the south

3   Crag Lough from the east

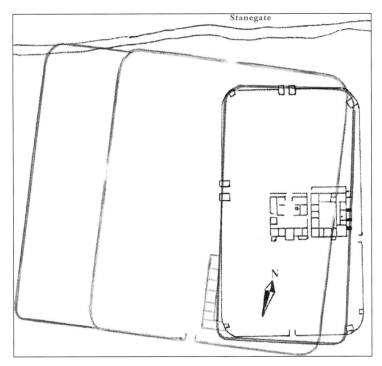

4   Vindolanda's
     successive forts:
     Period I is shown
     red, Periods II-III
     green, Period IV
     blue, the late stone
     fort black

5   Excavation in the deep levels in
     the 1980s

6   *Excavation in the deep levels in 1991*

7   *Excavation in the deep levels in 2001: one of the outer western ditches of Period I, with later timber buildings subsiding above it*

8   The hoard of unused Samian from the innermost western ditch of Period I

Obverse   *Reverse*

*9   Trajan and Hadrian:
coins found at
Vindolanda*

10 *The horse's chamfron found in the Period III praetorium*

11 *A replica of the chamfron*

12 *Flavius Cerialis writing a
letter: an imaginary
portrayal by Susanna Birley.
His uniform is based on
that of a contemporary
fellow-officer, Flavius
Miccalus, on a relief from
Perinthus in Thrace*

13 *The early bath-house built for the Ninth Batavians: the tepidarium and caldarium
viewed from the west*

14 *A tile from the early bath-house marked by a pair of dog's paw-prints*

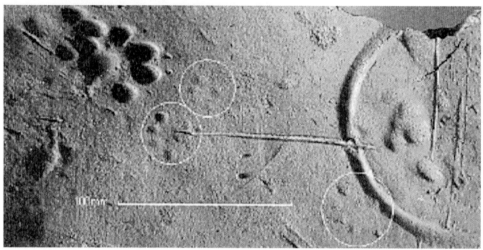

15 *A tile from the early bath-house with three faint cat prints (circled), a partly registered pair of dog prints and a faint dog print overlapping the C signature*

16 *A tile from the early bath-house with a cattle hoofprint*

17 *An undeciphered graffito on a tile from the early bath-house*

18 *The temple at the north-west end of the site, probably erected by the Ninth Batavians (during excavation in 2001)*

19 Altar to the God Magusanus (?)
found outside the temple

20 Decorative bronze head on a
heavy iron pin from the quarters
possibly erected for Hadrian

21 The start of a conventional excavation at the south-west corner of the stone fort in 1999

22 The praetorium *of the short-lived Severan fort*

23 Circular huts at the south-west corner of the later stone fort

24 Circular huts underlying the north wall of the later stone fort

25 The Vicus *main roadway viewed from the west*

26 *The* praetorium *of the stone fort from the south-west*

27 *The* principia *of the stone fort from the west. In the background Barcombe Hill*

28 Parts of a relief of the goddess Diana, reused as flooring in the late praetorium

29 The Lapidarium *in the museum garden: replicas of the altars found by Anthony Hedley*

30　*Robin Birley*

68   A letter from Haterius Nepos (Inv. 1379)

the lands of the Anavionenses and Selgovae. Rebuilding and reorganisation followed, from the Solway eastwards. The Stanegate may not have been called 'the frontier', but men stationed along it surely began to feel that they were at the very limits of empire. As for the Anavionenses and their neighbours, resentment at what had been inflicted on them may have begun to simmer, reaching boiling point when the news of Trajan's death (9 August, in the east) filtered through to Britain, by September 117. The Tungrians of Vindolanda had to fight the Britons again, perhaps for the first time in 30 years, not without losses, as the Vindolanda tombstone of T. Ann[ius] reveals (chapter 4). When Hadrian arrived in 122, he had just been in the German provinces, rigorously restoring military discipline there. Perhaps the regiments in northern Britain had been getting slack as well. *Disciplina* was featured on the imperial coinage. An altar, found in the North Tyne at Chesters, was set up 'To the Discipline of the Emperor Hadrian Augustus', *[d]iscipulinae imp. Had. Aug.*, by a cavalry regiment, the *ala Aug(usta) [o]b virt(utem) appel(lata)*, 'called Augustan because of its courage'.[23]

*69   The Anavion[enses] at
      Vindolanda: a fragment from
      a list (Inv. 1475A)*

6 The soldiers

The names of the soldiers

Some 200 (about half) of the persons named in the writing tablets may be identified as Batavian or Tungrian garrison-members or (a tiny handful) their women.[1] Almost all, it must be noted, have a single name, and were clearly not citizens. They would have to wait for this privilege until they had served 25 years. One or two in Period III, Sabinus (182), perhaps also Vatto (1475), are labelled *Trever*. This defined as them being from the Treveri, whose chief town was Augusta Treverorum (Trier) in Belgica. Further, Victor may have been labelled *Van[gio?]* (182), from the Suebian German Vangiones centred at Borbetomagus (Worms) in Upper Germany. This was presumably to distinguish these men from Batavians with the same name (Sabinus and Victor were certainly very common). About a dozen have names which, although previously unrecorded, look Germanic. The first part of Butimas means 'booty'. Chnisso and Chrauttius, beginning *Ch-* followed by a consonant, recall later Germanic names. (Note the Alamannic Chnodomarius and numerous Franks, Chlodovicus – Clovis – being the best known.) 'Sister Thuttena', greeted in Chrauttius' letter (310), has a name similar to Germanic ones beginning Thud- or Thiud-. Gambax may be from the Old High German word *gambar*, 'strenuous'. Hvepn[us] clearly means 'weapon'. Possibly Germanic are Albiso, Gamiso, Gannallius, Hvete[ ], Leubius, Onno[ ] and Sautenus. Some others, clearly not Latin, cannot be pinned down as either Germanic or Celtic: Ammius, Anveugus, Ucenius, Usarius and Vileus.

A few of the Batavians actually have Greek names: examples are Aristo (?), Ascanius, Cep(h)alio, Corinthus, Dardanus (?), Elpis – clearly a woman attached to a member of the regiment – Onesimus and Paris. In the Latin west such names generally indicated that their bearers were slaves or freedmen. But Greek names are found among the soldiers in the German imperial bodyguard in Julio-Claudian Rome, who included more Batavians than any other Germans in their ranks, and may have stayed in fashion among the Batavians after the old bodyguard was dissolved.[2]

Still, most of the Batavians and Tungrians have Celtic or Latin names, albeit some of the latter are 'Latinised' forms of native originals. Agilis, 'agile' in Latin, may be adapted from a Germanic name such as Agilo; Audax, meaning 'bold' in Latin, probably represented the Germanic word (attested in Gothic) *audags*, 'blessed'; Vindex, Latin for 'avenger', is probably an adaption of Celtic *vindos*, 'white, shining' – as in the name of Vindolanda itself. There is a good sprinkling of Celtic names.

Already attested elsewhere are: Andecarus, Atrectus, Atto, Billo, Buccus, Caledus, Catussa, Exomnius, Messicus, Uxperus, Vatto and Vattus. Acranius, Cessaucius, Settius, Suasco, Tagarminis, Troucisso, Varcenus, Viranus and Viriocius, even if not previously recorded, are clearly of Celtic type.

The majority of the men – and of the small number of women attested – have standard Latin names. These include well-known ones such as Amabilis, Atticus, Albanus, Albinus, Candidus, Capito, Celer, Crescens, Crispa and Crispus, Diligens, Felicio, Festus, Fidelis, Flavinus, Florus, Fortunatus, Fraternus, Fuscus, Germanus, Ingenuus, Januarius, Justinus, Lucanus, Lucius, Lupus, Macrinus, Mansuetus, Marcus, Masc(u)lus, Modius, Natalis, Paternus, Pol(l)io, Prudens, Quintus, Rufinus, Rufus, Sabinus, Sanctus, Saturninus, Senecio, Similis, Simplex, Sollemnis, Taurus, Taurinus, Tetricus, Valentinus, Verecunda and Verecundus, Victor and Vitalis. There are a few less common ones: Arcanus, Aventinus, Cogitatus, Culcianus, Equester, Fadus, Firmanus, Frumentius, Lucerius, Messor, Rhenus and Tullio, while Sequentinius, not previously attested, is of a type common in the Celtic provinces, 'fabricated' from Latin Sequentinus.

Names alone – in any case usually given by parents, or perhaps to new recruits by their officers – give limited insight into the self-identity of these men and women: did they see themselves as Romans or as Batavians and Tungrians? A letter found in a Period II level (1187) may be noted. At the end, the writer, probably a *cornic(u)larius* (senior NCO in the regimental headquarters) named Ascanius, first greets 'Verecunda and Sanctus, Lupus, Capito'. Then he adds 'and all friends and citizens, together with whom I pray that you are in good health'. This seems to attest a particular sense of solidarity among the Batavians – by 'citizens' Ascanius no doubt meant 'Batavian citizens' rather than 'Roman citizens'. Further, two documents suggest that all concerned felt themselves to be superior to the native Britons. The use of the derogatory or patronising word *Brittunculi* (164) is a clear pointer. So too is the outrage expressed by a man whom the centurions had beaten (344): he was not only 'innocent' but from 'overseas' – by implication he took it for granted that Britons so treated would have no grounds for protest.

Purchases by the soldiers

The life of the soldiers can be illustrated both by their letters and by the accounts listing what they had purchased. Nothing of this sort survives from Period I, but in Periods II to IV they are fairly abundant. Ascanius, who greeted 'all friends and citizens', does not have a very common name and is presumably the same man listed in a Period III account (183) as owing over 32 *denarii* for 90 pounds of iron. As he wrote the letter from elsewhere, he was perhaps on leave at the time or on an official journey. A letter to a soldier probably sent from his home in the Batavian country (346) refers to socks, underpants and sandals being dispatched to him, some of them from a person or place called Sattua, and ends with greetings for several named *contubernales*, messmates or comrades, 'with whom I pray that you may live very happily'. The legible names include Elpis, surely a woman, Tetricus and perhaps Rhenus.

Other, larger items of clothing were probably ordered by the regimental commander's office and in at least one case apparently obtained from the continent. [Cl]odius Super begins his letter to Cerialis (255): 'I am glad that our Valentinus has duly approved the clothing on his return from Gaul'. Super goes on to put in a bid for cloaks and tunics 'which my boys need'. Although only a centurion (it seems), he calls Cerialis not only 'Lord', *domine*, but also *frater carissime*, 'dearest brother', in the closing greeting. Still, in view of his two names he was presumably a Roman citizen. If the Batavian units were still recruited in the traditional fashion, perhaps he was also a member of the Batavian aristocracy, content to accept a position as centurion in the first instance, with prospects of becoming a prefect later. The final sentence of his letter (before the greeting) remains slightly enigmatic. It might refer to his just having joined the Ninth Batavians: 'You know, for sure, that I am justified in asking for this [i.e. an issue of clothing for 'my boys'], since I am a man of the Ninth (*cum sim nonanus*), having also obtained my transfer (*etiam adep[tus] translationem*).'[3]

Two accounts list goods supplied by a man called Gavvo, one (207) exclusively of cloaks and tunics (of various kinds) and capes (?), the numbers of garments involved ranging from two to 15. They were to be issued to the men, rather than being intended for the prefect's household. A tablet from Period III or IV (1210), on which the names of 12 men are listed, is described on the back as '*[r]atio vestis*', 'clothing account'. Whether the men had to purchase these items at a marked-up price is not clear. It may be significant that another document (178) lists *reditus castelli*, 'revenues of the fort': it covers five days, from 27 to 31 July, with takings totalling over 80 *denarii*. The garrison clearly had things to sell – as the letters to Cassius Saecularis referring to sale of barley (213) and perhaps also of timber (215) indicate.

Several accounts give a good idea of what the men were purchasing. One (1326) shows that several men, including a decurion, had bought something described as

70 [Cl]odius Super writes to the C.O. (255)

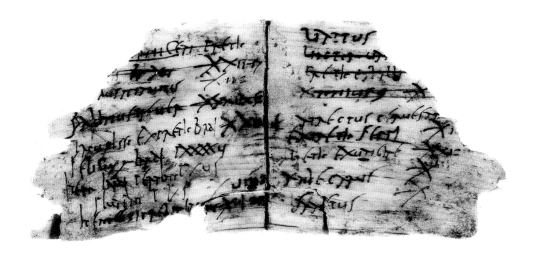

71 An account from Period III (182)

being 'of glass' (*vitreum*), and other purchases included a platter (*scutula*) and a
cooking-kettle (*cucuma*). Only one name is preserved, that of Firmanus, and it is in
the genitive: unfortunately it remains unknown whether the reference was to a man
'in the century of Firmanus', to a slave of his – or to his girlfriend, who might have
been listed as his 'messmate' (cf. below on Tagamas).

   In a detailed account (182), almost certainly for men of the Ninth Batavians
(although found in a Period IV level), the entries were struck through in some cases,
clearly when the items had been paid for. The surviving part begins with a bugler
(*cornicen*) – name missing – who had paid his bill of over 12 *denarii* but still owed two
denarii and two *asses* 'for sundries'. Sabinus the Treveran had paid up his 38.5 *denarii*
and two *asses* for unspecified purchases. Troucisso[4] still owed '13.5 *denarii* as part of
the price for bacon', the centurion Felicio owed 'eight *denarii* and two *asses* for 45
pounds of bacon, and 15 pounds of lard', while the book-keeper recorded receiving
from him six *denarii* and two and three-quarters *asses* 'for sundries'. Other men listed
include Vattus, Victor – who had bought a horse – the centurion Exomnius, the
brewer Atrectus, Andecarus, Sanctus, Sautenus and Varianus. Felicio may have
bought the large quantity of bacon and lard on behalf of his century. Another
account (193) shows him buying on credit (*mutuo*) spices, gruel and 160 eggs –
perhaps two each for the 80 men under him? Other items of food are registered in
various fragmentary tablets: a chicken, onions and olives (1476) in one, beet, eggs,
beans, pulse in another (1529). Further, it seems that the soldiers sometimes
purchased chickens and geese from the prefect (1474A, cf. chapter 6, below).

   A Period IV account (181) shows Candidus having bought firewood and a tunic,
while unspecified purchases by Tetricus, Primus, Alio the vet and Vitalis the bath-man
are listed, evidently as having been paid. There follows the entry *reliqui debent*, 'the rest

owe': Ingenu(u)s, seven *denarii*, Acranius three and then a group, *equites Vardulli*, 'the Vardullian cavalry', owing seven *denarii*. These troopers had presumably been detached from their parent regiment, the *cohors I fida Vardullorum equitata*, to provide a cavalry backing for the entirely infantry First Tungrians. The entry for the Vardulli is followed by a debt of three *denarii* for *contubernalis Tagamatis vexsillari*, literally 'the messmate of the flag-bearer Tagamas', who is likely to have been serving with the Vardulli – and his 'messmate' may well have been an unnamed girlfriend. Although the presence of women is clearly recognisable archaeologically, for example by female shoes, women other than officers' wives do not occur very often in the tablet. It may be recalled that the writer of the 'underpants' letter greeted Elpis, whose name is unmistakably female, along with other 'messmates', one Verecunda was greeted in a Period II letter (1108), and that from Chrauttius to Veldedeius greets 'sister Thuttena'. A very fragmentary account from Period III (187) registers a small sum of money owed by *Crispa Polionis*, 'Polio's Crispa'. Greetings for Ingenua and Varranilla (?) in a letter about spare roofing material (1578) have been mentioned in the previous chapter.

An account (186) found in a Period IV level, datable by mention of the consuls for the year 111, written between December 110 and February 111, shows three men presumably from the Tungrians, Gracilis, Audax and Similis, registering a variety of goods, with quantities and prices. In one case, the item, 100 *clavos caligares*, boot-nails, costing two *asses*, was for Gracilis. The other entries register items booked or obtained 'through' one of the three: over 85 pounds of salt, and two kinds of meat, evidently goat and pork. Further, on two occasions, shortly before the New Year and again in February, a *metretes* of *cervesa*, beer, is listed. The *metretes* was a measure containing 100 *sextarii*, the equivalent of about 50 pints, and the cost was only eight *asses*. This early variety of beer was brewed without hops and hence did not keep for long. No doubt it was often brewed from barley, but beer was also produced from a cereal called *bracis*, which is mentioned several times in the tablets. The Tungrians, like the Batavians, who seem to have had their own regimental brewer, clearly consumed beer regularly, in large quantities.

Boot-nails also feature in a Period III account (1528C-E), with purchases by men from the Batavians: Taurinus bought 350 on 20 July, while Tetricus needed only six

72 *Soldiers' boots*

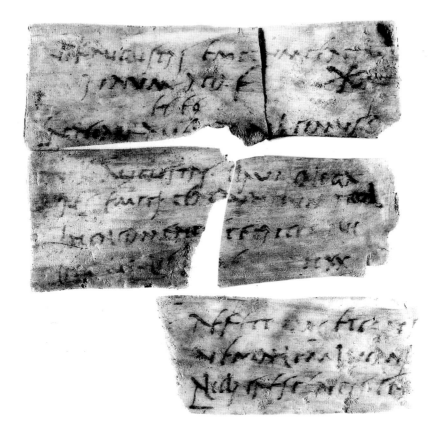

73   Batavians buying new nails for their boots (clavi caliga/res, line 5/6: Inv. 1528C)

nails *in calciamentis*, 'in footwear', and 20 *in galliculis*, 'in Gallic shoes'. Later entries show Prudens receiving 30 nails for his *campagones*, yet another kind of footwear, on 13 August, while Taurinus needed nine nails for his *galliculi*, and, also for this kind of shoe, Lucanus needed 12 and Aventinus 11 nails. It seems rather remarkable that purchases of such small numbers of nails were painstakingly recorded. It is not recorded what they cost, but presumably the price was much the same as for Gracilis' nails, one *as* for 50.

The same account also records Taurinus buying *acia*, thread, presumably to repair his clothing, while Lucanus had paid to have his belt or cummerbund, *ventralem*, repaired and re-stitched, *refectum et cons[utum]*, and Crescens' shirt, *alicla*, is referred to, perhaps also having been repaired. Again, no trace has survived of what they paid – nor is it clear whom they paid. 'Gallic shoes' crop up again in another tablet (1320), which also mentions two British products, both unfortunately too fragmentary to identify, although one might be tunics or shoes. Another fragment (1322A) registered at least seven men – none of their names survive complete – receiving 'pairs' of something, *par[ia]*, probably footwear. By contrast,

74 Purchases in Period V (184)

on another fragment (1319), over 20 lines long, a good many names survive, including that of Lucanus and, probably, Felicio, and dates, in April and May, but the only legible purchase seems to be beans, *fabae*.

Taurinus' name is the only one preserved in another tablet (1478B-C). Between five and nine pounds of bronze are registered as being 'left by [or for] Taurinus'. There follow 'lantern, repaired' and – once again – 'nails'. Another fragment lists 'a second bolt, for a bread-bin', 'two repaired skillets', 'dog-collars', another bolt, and something to do with a 'cross-beam for a suspended wagon', the term *pensilis covinni* being rather surprising: *covinnus*, which occurs again in other, very fragmentary tablets, is otherwise only recorded as the name for the Gallic and British scythed war-chariot, which can hardly be in question here.

One of the latest tablets, to judge from its findspot in a Period V level, is an account (184) listing items purchased by men in the centuries of Ucenius and Tullio, presumably in the First Tungrians. The items listed are fairly miscellaneous: two *denarii* worth of pepper bought by Gambax son of Tappo, blankets or overcoats bought by Tagarminis for at least 13 *denarii*, a cloak costing five *denarii* and three *asses* bought by Lucius the shield-maker, *corrigia*, shoe-laces, costing two and a half *denarii*, bought by Butimas, and an undershirt or vest (*subarmal[um?]*), purchased by [C]aledus. Otherwise the account seems to concern principally things that the men might have used in the baths: towels or 'sweat-cloths', *sudaria*, which occur at least five times, a flask, a 'buskin', *cothurnus*, quite likely a wooden sandal used for walking in the hottest room of the baths – tallow or grease, *sebum*, is also mentioned at least five times, being perhaps a substitute for olive oil, for a massage after the bath. The large new bath-house constructed by the Batavians during Period III certainly continued in use after that fort had been demolished and rebuilt, as a major form of relaxation for the garrison.

Letters from friends and family

Two soldiers' letters show how important it was for the men to get news from their friends. One (311), from a man called Sollemnis to his 'brother', i.e. comrade, Paris, opens with a half-joking but obviously seriously meant complaint that Paris had not written to him:

> So that you may know that I am in good health, which I hope you are in turn, you most irreligious fellow, who haven't even sent me a single letter – but I think I am behaving in a more civilised way by writing to you!

The main subject of the letter is missing, but the ending survives: 'you are to greet my messmate Diligens from me and Cogitatus and Corinthus, and I ask you to send me the names . . . Farewell, dearest brother.' The address on the back reveals that Paris was in the Third Cohort of Batavians, and possibly names his fort, 'at Ulucium, in the fort (?*Ulucio cas[tris]*). This name also crops up as the place where a soldier wished to spend his leave (174, cf. chapter 4). A fragment of a letter to a man called Fadus (321) probably contains an even more pointedly worded reproach to a non-

75 Sollemnis complains that Paris hasn't written (311)

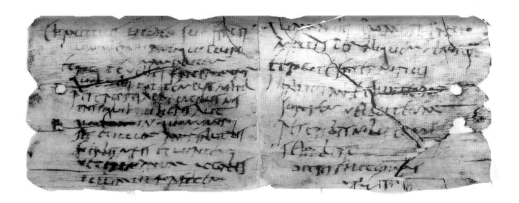

76   Chrauttius' letter to Veld(ed)eius (310). For the address see **27**

replier: it begins 'I hope that it may turn out badly for you' – and perhaps continued
on the lines of 'unless you at last write back'.

   Much more informative is a complete letter (310) from a man with the very
Germanic name Chrauttius, 'to his brother and old messmate Veldeius' – the latter's
name being spelt 'Veldedeius' in the address on the back. Once again, the writer
begins with a reproach:

> And I ask you, brother Veldeius – I am surprised that you have not written
> anything back to me for such a long time – whether you have heard
> anything from our kinsmen, or about Quotus – in which unit he is – and
> you are to greet him in my own words – and Virilis the vet. You are to
> ask him whether you may send through one of our people the shears
> which he promised me for a price. And I ask you, brother Virilis, that you
> greet from me sister Thuttena and write back to us about Velbuteius, how
> he is. I wish you may be very happy. Farewell.

There is a problem of interpretation about the address on the back: *Londini.
Veledeio equisione co(n)s(ularis) a Chrauttio fratre*, 'At London. To Veldedeius,
groom of the consular (governor), from Chrauttius, (his) brother'. If Veldedeius
were the governor's groom, it would be natural for him to have been serving at
London. The reason why the letter ended up at Vindolanda could readily be
explained: Veldedeius had brought it with him – and indeed, not far from where
it was found a large leather offcut was discovered, on which was scratched
VELDEDII SPONDE. This is surely yet another spelling of his name, and
Spondé might conceivably be the name of his horse, or mare, 'Veldedius'
Spondé'. He was also, it is clear, the owner of the fine, richly decorated horse's
chamfron found in the *praetorium*, near the piece of leather with his name on it.
It was evidently made for him here – which suggests that his stay was fairly

lengthy – and comparison of the champion with modern horses' heads suggests that his mare was of high quality: it fits best a pure bred Arab mare of 15.1 hands.[5] Chrauttius might then have been a soldier in the Ninth Batavians, in which, as 'an old messmate', Veldedeius had no doubt served before being chosen to join the governor's staff. Now he was back – probably accompanying the governor, whose presence at Vindolanda is recorded on another tablet (1474, cf. below chapter 4).

On the other hand, the natural interpretation of 'at London' is that this is the place where the letter was written. For one thing, several other letters found at Vindolanda carry the names of places other than Vindolanda in the locative, and it is difficult to imagine that they were all brought back from elsewhere. In that case, Chrauttius – who could have been serving there in the governor's *singulares*, guards – wrote the letter at London to Veldedeius while the latter was on his travels. Either way, the odds are that the two men had served together in the Ninth Batavians. If Chrauttius was at London, one must assume that Virilis, Velbuteius and 'sister' Thuttena were friends whom he assumed that Veldedeius would be meeting on his journey north. If 'at London' refers to the destination of the letter, these three will no doubt also have been there – and there is no way of guessing where Chrauttius was based. Be this as it may, Veldedeius might have died while still in the north. At any rate, a tombstone found not far away from Vindolanda, of which the funerary formula, *[Dis M]anibus* written out in full, ought to be fairly early, commemorated a man called 'Vilidedius', perhaps yet another spelling of his name.[6]

Another, rather fragmentary letter (312), with the same kind of problematic locative place-name in the address, is headed on the back *Coris*, 'at Coria (Corbridge)'. It was written to Cessaucius Nigrinus (?), who is labelled *dup.*, i.e. *dup(licarius)*, a 'double-pay man' or NCO, by a man called Tullio. The surviving part reads:

> I ask you to come to him as soon as you can, for we regard him as a friend (?). About the things which you have sent me, I see no reason (?) why he should know . . . you had written . . . I owe you ten *denarii* . . . (Greet from me) Candidus and Natalis . . . I ask you to send me some . . . I ask you to give Viriocius a warm welcome. I pray that you may have good health. Farewell.

Several other letters written to members of the garrison show that money was a major concern, sometimes much larger sums than Tullio's ten *denarii* – and not all debtors were so ready to repay as Tullio was. A loan was clearly the subject of the letter from Ascanius, the surviving part of which begins: 'that he should send back my 250 (?) *denarii*, which I entrust to the cognisance of his prefect.' Presumably a fellow-soldier – probably in a different unit – to whom he had lent money had failed to pay it back and Ascanius had to bring the matter to the attention of the man's commanding officer. Another long letter (1297+1528A-B; Period III) from a soldier, or perhaps rather an NCO, evidently concerns a dispute about an even larger sum, 2000 *denarii*. The writer affirms his own integrity and stresses that the matter can be sorted out 'with the goldsmiths and silversmiths' – which might, in practice, have meant 'with the moneylenders'. He further insists that 'you should know that I will not withdraw from our *contubernium* (shared quarters in the barrack) or from the *scola* (a club-house for NCOs)'. He ends with greetings for Rhenus, Felicio, Tetricus and Crescens. Rhenus and Tetricus were also among those greeted in the 'underpants' letter (346).

A man called Lucius is the recipient of two letters. One, found in a Period III level (300), which suggests that he was serving with the Ninth Batavians, mentions that the writer, whose name is missing, has 'sent back [. . .] and Frontinus the cavalrymen to the camp on 26 February', and concludes by remarking ' . . . so that you might know, I have written to you. I hope, brother, that you may enjoy good health, farewell.' The other letter (299), although found in a Period V level, may be to the same man – albeit the name was very common – this time with part of the address being preserved: of the writer's name only ...TERI survives, but the addressee is labelled *Lucio decurion[i]*, 'to Lucius the decurion'. The surviving text opens: 'which is the principal reason for my letter – that you are fit (literally 'brave', *fortis*).' The writer goes on to report that 'a friend has sent me 50 oysters from Cordonovi. In order that . . . more rapidly . . . ' – one wonders whether he added, for example, 'of which I am sending you half'. A letter from Arcanus to Marinus (1351) refers to Arcanus having bought something and may then mention someone having given him some money – the word *denarium* follows. On the second sheet he tells Marinus that 'I have sent you a little lamp (*lucernulam*) through . . . ' and ends with greetings for, among others, 'Crescens and Florentinus and [all your – or our] messmates.'

A woman called Ingenua has already been mentioned, who was evidently at Vindolanda. An Ingenua who might be the same person is mentioned in what was probably a draft letter (1575), from a Period III or IV level, liberally spattered with spelling mistakes, written by a man called Florus. He wrote to someone called Caltavirus (or perhaps Ealtavirus), who was evidently the father of his female companion:

> The locked box and whatever things are locked inside it, you should give [*dabes*, instead of *dabis*] to .am.us the *beneficarius* [this word, in the dative, is misspelled *benifeciario*], which he will seal with his ring . . . and do not give it to him unless he puts it into a wagon immediately. Ingenua greets you, your daughter ['your' and 'you' are both plural, *vestra* and *vos*, which by implication means that Florus was greeting his correspondent's wife as well].'

This was followed by the words 'Give to Caltavirus' (again, *dabes* is written instead of *dabis* – and earlier Florus had written *signabet* instead of *signabit* for 'he will seal'). On a second sheet Florus drafted a letter to his 'brother' Titus. 'Brother' is misspelled *frates* instead of *frater*; and the spelling *dabes* for *dabis*

77 Florus drafts a letter
   to Ingenua's father
   (Inv. 1575)

78 *Florus drafts a letter to*
Titus (Inv. 1575)

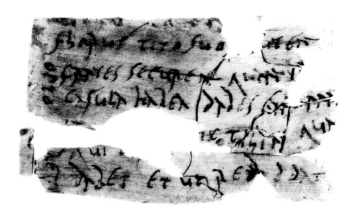

79 *An account for Florus (Inv. 1316)*

recurs, likewise *dabet* instead of *dabit*; and he wrote *habea* instead of *habes*. Once again, the letter is concerned with transport of objects:

> You are to give the axe which you have in your cottage, *casula*, to G . . . who has some dishes which he will give to you, and in order that he may give back . . . I pray that you are in good health.

An account (1316), which perhaps belongs to the writer of these letters, for it is headed *ratio Flori*, was found in a Period III level, but may possibly include a consular date for AD 107, which would put it early in Period IV. It begins in late December, and registers Florus receiving nails, *cla[vos]*, pork-fat on 1 January, and a few days later nails again.

Two writing tablets from the centurion's quarters

By far the most detailed account (180) was found in the centurion's quarters of the Period IV barrack. It is a *ratio frumenti em[ensi]*, 'account of measured out wheat', covering three pages, a total of 38 lines. Amounts of wheat are registered, in *modii* – a *modius* being eight and three-quarter litres dry measure – allocated in September, probably in AD 121, to individuals and to groups. The man who wrote the account was probably a civilian supplier, indeed a member of a family firm, as can be inferred from several entries. The first reads: 'from that which I myself have put into the barrel, *[ex quo] ipse dedi in cupam*, for myself, for bread'; the quantities are not preserved. Other entries register an allocation of '19 *modii* in three sacks, for father', and 'father' is listed again further down, receiving two *modii*, and on a third occasion, this time specifying that he was *ad j[uv]encos*, 'at

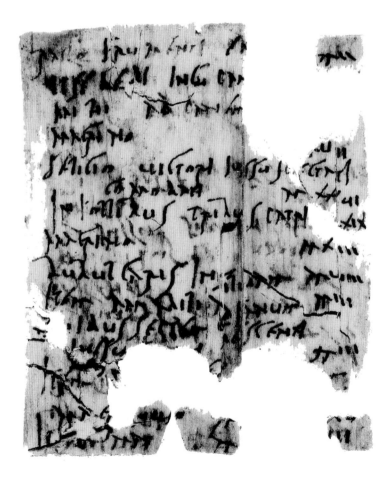

80   The first sheet of the wheat account (the bubulcari are in line 9: 180)

(i.e. in charge of?) the bullocks'. Besides this, four separate entries register allo-cations *tibi*, 'for you' – perhaps the writer's brother, or wife? One is 'for twisted loaves, two *modii*', *ad turtas m.ii*, another for wheat (the quantity is missing) in a 'sack', *in folle*, followed by the word *br.gese*, perhaps 'a bag from Briga', the name of a fort mentioned twice in other tablets (190, 292); the amounts assigned in the remaining two entries 'for you' are missing.

Most, if not all, of the remaining recipients seem to be members of the garrison. The listing begins:

> For Macrinus, seven *modii*; for Felicius Victor, by order of Spectatus, 26
> *modii* allocated; for Macrinus, 13 *modii*; for the oxherds in the wood, eight
> *modii*; likewise, for Amabilis, at the temple (*fanum*), three *modii*.

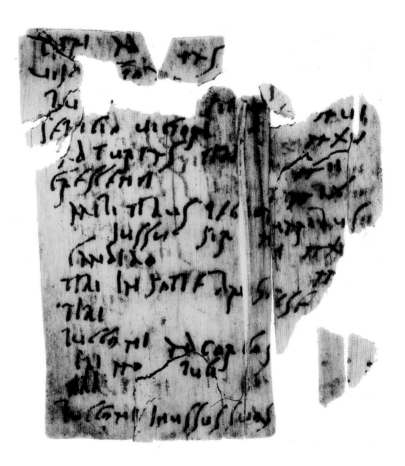

*81   The second sheet of the wheat account (*Lucconi ad porcos, *four lines from the bottom: 180)*

The oxherds would be looking after the baggage-animals close to the fort. Amabilis was perhaps a soldier assigned to guard the temple, which may well have been the one located outside the western end of the fort and evidently built by the Batavians for their chief god, Magusanus (see chapter 7). There is no reason why the Tungrians should not have kept up the shrine. After the entry for Amabilis comes the first date, probably 31 August or 1 September, with an allocation to Crescens 'by order of Firmus'. On 26 September a *beneficiarius* whose name began Lu- received six *modii*, Felicius Victor another 15, Crescens nine, 'the legionary soldiers, by order of Firmus' between 11 and 14. Further amounts were issued to 'Lucco, in charge of the pigs', 'Primus, (slave?) of Lucius' – Lucius was perhaps the *beneficiarius* Lu- mentioned above – and 'for Lucco, for his own use'. One further entry registers 'likewise for myself, for bread' and finally the total is summed up as being 320.5 *modii*. No payments are registered. It may perhaps be inferred that these corn dealers had been paid in advance under contract. A feature of special interest is the mention of legionary soldiers. Their presence may be a pointer to preparations being in hand to build Hadrian's Wall, a task primarily for legionaries. These men were perhaps an advance party, who had to be housed somewhere. Later on large numbers of temporary camps were constructed, some very close to Vindolanda.

Another tablet, found in close proximity to the wheat-account, is the longest of all the letters (343). It was written on two folding diptychs, making four pages in all, possibly early in AD 122, by a man called Octavius. His description of his own activities makes him sound like another civilian trader, although it is not impossible that he was, for example, an NCO or centurion with commissariat duties. He wrote to a man called Candidus, clearly in a great hurry – he folded the letter together before the ink was dry – and in a state of some agitation. The address on the back simply has the place-name, abbreviated, *Vindol*. On the basis that place-names on the back of letters indicate the place of writing, this may mean that Octavius came to Vindolanda, hoping to talk to Candidus. Finding that his friend was away, he hurriedly wrote the letter before pressing on (cf. also chapter 1, *Addresses*). Another unusual feature of the letter – the longest yet found at Vindolanda – is that Octavius began it on the right-hand sheet and continued on the left, in each case, contrary to the standard practice. The reason may be that he was left-handed. It must also be noticed that his standard of Latinity is unusually poor in comparison with the great majority of letters and documents from Vindolanda.[7] This remarkable piece deserves to be quoted in full:

> As to the 100 pounds of sinew from Marinus – I will settle up. From when you wrote about this he has not even mentioned it to me. I have written to you several times that I have bought ears of grain, about 5000 *modii*, on account of which I need *denarii* – unless you send me something, at least 500 *denarii*, I will lose what I have given as a down payment, about 300 *denarii*, and will be embarrassed, so I ask you: send me some *denarii* as soon as possible. The hides which you write are at Cataractonium – write that they be given to me – and the wagon you write about – and write to me

what is with that wagon. I would have collected them already – except that I did not care to wear out the baggage-animals while the roads are bad. See with Tertius about the eight and a half *denarii* which he got from Fatalis – he has not credited them to my account.

Know that I have finished 170 hides and I have 119 *modii* of threshed *bracis*. Make sure that you send me *denarii* so that I can have ears of grain on the threshing-floor – besides, I have already threshed whatever I had.

A messmate of our friend Frontius has been here. He wanted me to allocate him hides and was to give *denarii* – I said to him I would give him the hides by 1 March, he decided he would come on 13 January, but did not turn up and took no trouble to get them as he had hides. If he had given the money, I was going to give him them.

I hear that Frontinius Julius has on sale at a high price leather-ware which he bought here for five *denarii* apiece.

Greet Spectatus and Januarius and Firmus. I have had a letter from Gleuco.

Needless to say, the original has neither paragraphing nor punctuation.

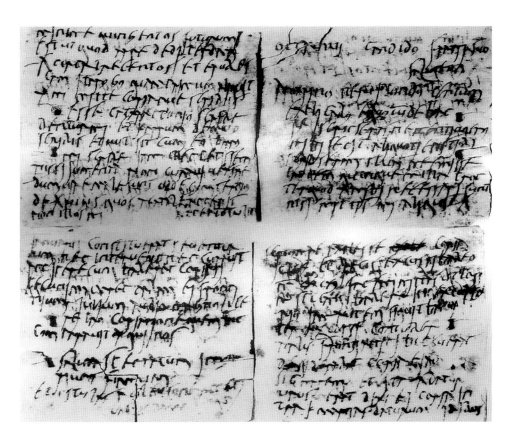

82   The letter from Octavius to Candidus (343)

The large quantity of sinew supplied by Marinus was presumably to make sinew cord, used among other things for military catapults. The other items, grain, including *bracis*, and hides, are in such large quantities as to suggest that Octavius had a contract to supply the army. This, combined with the evidence for legionaries being stationed at Vindolanda, may mean that large-scale preparations were being made to cater for the legions that would shortly begin building the Wall.

Spectatus and Firmus may be the same men by whose 'order' wheat was allocated, and they could well have been legionary centurions – as could Candidus, Tertius, Fatalis, Januarius and Gleuco.[8] The names Candidus and Tertius are attested as those of centurions in charge of building parts of the Wall, but both names are extremely common. Octavius' Candidus may at least be the same man as the Candidus in the wheat account. It is also worth noting that another centurion whose name is recorded on a Wall building stone was called Octavius Seranus.[9] Fatalis is an extremely rare name, so there is a good chance that this might be the same man as Tiberius Claudius Fatalis. He came from Rome itself, and served twice in the Isca (Caerleon) legion II Augusta, with a spell in XX Valeria Victrix based at Deva (Chester) in between, and went on to service in two separate Danube legions and one in Cappadocia, before dying at the age of 42 at Jerusalem, by then in the legion X Fretensis. He might also be the Fatalis who wrote a letter (349) to Vindolanda in Period IV.[10]

Centurions did not normally retire from the army after 25 years' service – some went on until they were over 80. Hence it would not be surprising if Gleuco and Firmus were identical with centurions attested over 20 years later, on the Antonine Wall in Scotland. Gleuco's name is spelled there slightly differently, to be sure, 'Glico'. Firmus might be the remarkable Marcus Cocceius Firmus, who dedicated no fewer than seven altars to a large variety of deities at Auchendavy. He in turn has been identified with the centurion Cocceius Firmus, owner of a woman slave sentenced for some crime to labour in a salt-works, kidnapped from there by 'barbarian brigands', sold by them and then resold: the case was immortalised in the *Digest* of Roman law, which records that Firmus was repaid the money from her sale.[11]

What gives the wheat account added interest is that two out of the three tablets were reused on the back for a draft letter of protest (344) – written by the same man who wrote the account. He had evidently been severely 'beaten with rods', in fact 'beaten until I bled'. The reason had something to do with goods, *mercem*, which his persecutor had apparently 'poured away'. It could be inferred that a centurion had pronounced that some form of liquid goods – perhaps wine or olive oil – which the unfortunate man had supplied were of unacceptable quality and had simply 'poured them down the drain'. The letter proceeds

> As befits an honest man I implore Your Majesty not to allow me, an innocent man, to have been beaten with rods and, my Lord, since I could not complain to the prefect, because he was detained by ill-health, I complained, but to no avail, to the *beneficiarius* and to the [?other] centurions in the regiment. I implore Your Clemency not to suffer a man from overseas and an innocent one to have been made to bleed by a beating, as though I had committed some crime.

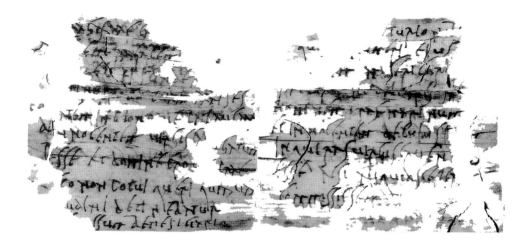

83   The draft protest by the man the centurions had flogged (344)

That the appeal was addressed to 'Your Majesty' and 'Your Clemency' is very striking. Given that the tablet was found in the centurion's quarters of the barrack of Period IV, the end of which is datable on archaeological evidence to *c.*120, it suggests that the victim was hoping to present a petition to the Emperor Hadrian in person, whose arrival was no doubt awaited in early summer 122 – he probably arrived at latest in early July, to supervise the construction of his Wall.[12]

Hadrian, by then been emperor for nearly five years, made a feature of his accessibility to individuals of all classes. That he would be expected at Vindolanda makes good sense: it was the obvious base from which to inspect the central sector of the line for his new frontier work. Indeed a particularly high-quality building, with painted wall-plaster, was erected in the middle of the fort just at this time (cf. chapter 4). The appellant insists that as 'a man from overseas' – *tra(n)smarinus* – as well as an innocent one he should not have been beaten. This casts an indirect but very instructive light on attitudes to the 'natives' – the implication is that a Briton *could* have been beaten without hesitation. However, the fact that the draft was found in the centurion's quarters may suggest that it was confiscated and that the writer never had the chance to hand a fair copy to the Emperor.

Major's letter and *chirografi*

Another possible civilian trader is a man called Major. A letter (1022), probably from Period IV rather than III, which he wrote to a man called Cocceiius Maritimus – with the name, normally spelt just Cocceius, indicating someone whose citizenship was owed to the Emperor Nerva – is also worth quoting in full, not least since it is virtually complete:[13]

84   Major's letter to Maritimus (Inv. 1022)

I want you to know that a letter has been sent to me from my father, in which he writes to me that I should let him know what I have done about (the grain) that has been poured out (*fussa*). As to which, if you have had dealings on this with the Caesariani, see that you write back to me clearly, so that I can write back to this effect to my father. If you have made an interim payment, I will issue (?) grain (*bracem*) to you straightaway, in proportion to the sum – let this be done.

   While I am writing this to you, I am making the bed warm. I wish that you may be very happy. My father (?) greets you. Farewell.

At the side of the second sheet he added a PS:

If you are going to send a boy to me, send a note of hand (*chir[ografum]*) with him, so that I may be safer.

The address on the back has the locative place-name *Vindoland(a)e* at the top left, 'at Vindolanda'. If the view here favoured is correct, that the place-name in this position refers to the place of writing, one must of course ask why the letter was not sent. In this case, Major's engaging statement that he was 'making the bed warm while writing', in other words, writing the letter in bed, provides a clue. This probably resulted in the ink-blotches spattered about the text. Hence it would have been understandable if a fair copy was made and sent, and this version retained.

   The 'Caesariani', 'Caesar's men', were slaves and freedmen of the emperor, employed empire-wide in administrative and, especially, tax-collecting duties. The word *fussa*, meaning literally 'poured out', can be understood to refer to the *bracis* which is mentioned later. Perhaps it had been sent by Major's father from overseas, and import duty, *portorium*, levied by the Caesariani, had been due on it, which Maritimus, Major's business partner or agent, had paid out on Major's behalf. One of the Caesariani may the Optatus, freedman or slave of the emperor (*Au[g. libertus* or *servus]*), who wrote, from Eburacum, a wax-tablet to someone whose name began Mo- at Vindolanda (1220). The name Optatus is not uncommon, but a fragmentary letter (1110) beginning 'Montanus to his Optatus', was possibly a draft reply.

The 'boy' may be assumed to be a slave. What he was to bring, the word translated 'note of hand', *chirografum*, crops up in several tablets. A letter (1131), found in a Period IV level, written, by coincidence or not, 'to Lord Optatus' – if this was the man in the stylus tablet he must have been an imperial freedman rather than slave, one imagines, to be addressed as *dominus* – from an unknown correspondent begins: 'Just as you wrote, I have asked (the question) and Flavius . . . licus . . . We have submitted a note of hand concerning the horse . . . '. Another letter (1254), from Period III or IV, from . . . us Aemilianus to Severinus, begins with a conventional remark: 'I have not neglected the opportunity offered, my Lord [of writing to you] . . . '. The second sheet refers to a 'note of hand from Velus' and to 'Saturninus' estimates'.

A few examples of such legal documents may be identified, written on stylus or wax tablets, more substantial than the wafer-thin ink leaf-tablets, and more durable if they had to be filed. One (Inv.725), perhaps registering a loan, is dated 19 January 98 (the 'fourth consulship of the Emperor Nerva') and concerned 'M . . . , son of . . . [name and patronymic illegible], soldier in the Ninth Cohort of Batavians, in the century of Aprilis'. A stylus tablet from Period V (1228), the text of which is totally illegible, nonetheless reveals its contents by an entry written in ink on the rim: 'Billo, in the century of S . . . , owes . . . ', *debet Billo 7 S . . .* This is one of several ink rim inscriptions identifiable on stylus tablets. They show

85 A partly legible stylus tablet: a loan on 19 January AD 98 (Inv. 725)

86   A rim inscription on a stylus tablet: Billo owes money (Inv. 1228)

that such tablets could be placed on end in a box or indeed a filing cabinet, and readily consulted. Finally, part of another stylus tablet (1112), also from Period V, registers some transaction involving *Aprilis Augusti*, perhaps an imperial slave also called – by coincidence – Aprilis, 'done at London (*actum Londini*) on the day before the Ides of August (12 August)'.

87   Part of a contract on a stylus tablet: 'Done at London on 12 August' (Inv. 1112)

7 The officers and their families[1]

Julius Verecundus

A few tablets survive, apart from the strength report of the First Tungrians, that give a little insight into the life of its commander in Period I, Julius Verecundus. These two names, incidentally, are both extremely common, but nothing would conflict with the hypothesis that he was a member of the Tungrian aristocracy. A letter (302) addressed probably to a slave of his contains what may be called a shopping-list:

> Two *modii* of bruised beans, 20 chickens, 100 apples – if you can find nice-looking ones – 100 or 200 eggs, if they are on sale there at a fair price . . . *mulsum* [honey-flavoured wine] . . . eight *sextarii* [about four litres] of fish-sauce (*muria*) . . . a *modius* of olives . . .

It may be supposed that the slave had been sent to Coria (Corbridge), or further afield, to purchase goods not available locally.

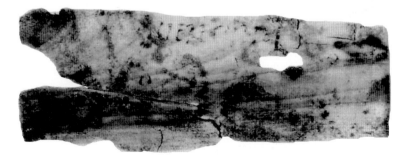

88 A shopping list for Verecundus' household (302)

A fragmentary letter, found in the Period I ditch (303), was written by Privatus to Albiso. Privatus is a typical slave's name, and on the address side Albiso's name, in the dative, is followed by the beginning of another name, just possibly Ve[recundi], which would indicate that Albiso was Verecundus' slave. The name may be Germanic, similar to that of the R. Elbe, *Albis*. None of the fragments gives connected sense, apart from the opening words *accepi superius*, 'I have received the upper . . . '.

Otherwise, there are only three not very informative scraps from letters to Verecundus himself. In one (210), from a colleague whose name ends –ius, the writer referred to 'my desire . . . nor has there yet been any more talk . . . ' and adds greetings from his wife, whose name is scarcely decipherable, perhaps 'my Flammula'. Another correspondent's letter (212) simply has the conventional opening, 'I have taken the opportunity of writing'. A third dealt with official business: 'I have understood (?) about this matter. Tomorrow I shall speak to . . . at Luguvalium. If you approve, come to me . . . '. Verecundus may have remained in the area with his regiment for some years after the Tungrians left Vindolanda. In a letter found in a Period III level (313) the writer refers to 'a priest, whom I ask that you send (?) to the prefect Verecundus about the festival (?)'. Another fragment (326) hints at problems: after mentioning a senator, whose name is fragmentary, but whose rank is clearly given by the abbreviation *c(larissimus) v(ir)*, 'right honourable man', probably a legionary legate rather than the governor, it continues with: 'you are in a rage about those soldiers (?) of Verecundus'.

Some prefects of the Ninth Batavians

It is not known who was commanding the Ninth Batavians when they arrived at Vindolanda, but there are at least three prefects who need to be fitted in before Flavius Cerialis: Veranius, Flavianus and Flavius Genialis. The first is known only by a fragmentary letter which gives his rank on the back as *praef(ecto) coh(ortis)*, from a man called something like Librinus (319). It could be, of course, that Veranius was the colleague called –ius who wrote to Verecundus: *cognomina* ending in –ius are not very common. Although an early governor of Britain was called Quintus Veranius, most Veranii in the north-western provinces do not owe their names to him. The name is favoured in the Rhineland, as a 'Latinisation' of a Celtic original. This prefect could well be a Batavian notable. As for Flavianus, he is firmly attested as prefect only by one

89   Flavianus wishes Cerialis a Happy New Year (261)

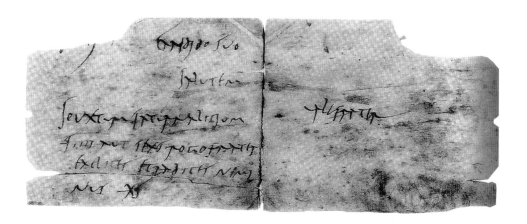

90   Genialis' slave Candidus is reminded about Saturnalia costs (301)

of the leave applications (172), but he is likely to be the same man as Hostilius Flavianus, who wrote to Cerialis (misspelling his name 'Cerealis') wishing him a 'Happy and Fortunate New Year' (261). His *cognomen* suggests that his mother was a Flavia, and one can guess that he too was a member of the Batavian elite. One other man may also be a prefect of the Ninth. Vettius Severus received a letter (305) from an unknown correspondent containing a request: 'you have, therefore, what I would wish to obtain from you. Write back to me . . . '. These few words hint that Severus enjoyed a position of authority, and in the address on the back his name is followed by what may be the remains of his title, *pr[aef]*, although the surviving letters are very faint.

Flavius Genialis

Flavius Genialis has already been mentioned in connection with the letter from Haterius Nepos, the census of the Anavionenses and the training of *Brittunculi*. Several tablets shed further light on this man, who, it may be inferred, was the immediate predecessor of Cerialis. Most of the letters to Genialis are mere fragments, three with the names of the writers, in two cases Flavius Proculus (219, 1337), probably the same man as the Proc[ulus] mentioned in Haterius Nepos' letter (1379), the other being Licinius Asper (224). An unknown correspondent sent him what looks like a letter of apology for not accepting an invitation (1424): ' . . . that I could not come, for a headache is affecting me very painfully' – the writer's wife was also suffering, it seems from the remaining traces. No information is available about Genialis' own wife, but several members of his household are on record.

A slave of Genialis, Candidus, received a letter (301) from another slave called Severus, no doubt, from the content, in December: 'Regarding the Saturnalia costs, I ask you, brother, to settle up at four or six *asses*, and radishes for not less than half a *denarius*.' If the word *radices* really does mean 'radishes', it must be admitted that this is a rather surprising request – but perhaps they were an important traditional part of Saturnalia fare. Apart from this, the spelling of the word, translated 'costs', as *souxtum*, instead of the normal *sumptum*, is remarkable; *ou* instead of *u* and the omission of an *m* after it are variants which are not uncommon in various parts of the Empire; *x*, representing the Celtic *ch-* sound, in place of *p*, shows that Severus was of Celtic origin.[2] The address gives the recipient very legibly as 'Candidus slave of Genialis the prefect', and Severus almost certainly described himself as a slave too, but the name of his owner is too faint to read. It ended –*i*, in the genitive, hence it was a man called –*us*, not –*is*. This means that Severus was not another slave of Genialis who had remained at home or elsewhere. That might have been the case with another possible slave of Genialis, Vegetus. The opening (and no more) is preserved of a letter from him to Genialis (1449): *Vegetus Geniali su[o]*, with, inserted on the line above, the word *domino*, hence: 'Vegetus to his Lord – or Master – Genialis'. He could, it is true, just have been a soldier under Genialis' command.

Genialis also had an ex-slave with him: another letter (1434) has the address *Gentili liberto Flavi Genialis*, 'to Gentilis, freedman of Flavius Genialis'.[3] This freedman is probably also the [–].tilis, writer of a letter to Genialis (217), who reported that 'I have sent (?) Crescens (to you) with . . . [someone or something]'. If so, he had been busy elsewhere on his patron's behalf. Gentilis was himself the recipient of a letter (1378) from a man called Suolcenus – perhaps another slave of Genialis? – who writes:

> Ingenus had approached me about the matter, which I strongly supported (?). I myself am not failing in my duty and I hope that I . . . I ask that you give me, through F . . . Ingenus has seen that I am not failing (in my duty?) concerning the wheels which I am waiting for. He will quickly arrange this. But I want you to collect the debt . . . The agreements in respect of the bond . . .

A letter to Genialis from an unknown correspondent (218) is more informative than the other scraps:

> I ask that, if there is anything you believe might be useful to me, you either send it or keep it on one side. As to what we need, I have sent word to you through our Paternus and Gavo. Thus anyone whom you had demanded I sent on to you at once.

Paternus is not identifiable, but Gavo, whose name was inserted in a different handwriting here, crops up in other tablets (197, 201) as a supplier of miscellaneous goods; he was probably civilian and perhaps a native Briton.

The names Flavius Genialis may be not uncommon, but they actually crop up at Rome together with those of Flavius Gentilis. A tombstone there registers the last resting-place of 'T. Flavius Gentilis, freedman of T. Flavius Genialis'.[4] This is at least a strong hint that the ex-prefect of Batavians and his household could have settled in the capital. For almost a century successive generations of Batavians had lived in Rome as members of the Julio-Claudian bodyguard. If, as here postulated, Genialis as well as Cerialis and the other commanders of the Ninth Batavians were themselves members of the Batavian aristocracy, they could easily have had relatives who had served in that unit, indeed they could have spent some of their own youth there – after the troubles of AD 68-70 had died down, some of the ex-bodyguards dismissed and sent by home by Galba may have returned to Rome. Two or three generations later, in AD 185, another man called Flavius Genialis, perhaps our man's grandson or great-grandson, was a tribune in the Praetorian Guard at Rome. He even became Guard Prefect eight years later – but was to hold office for a matter of weeks: he was appointed by Didius Julianus, whose reign only lasted from 28 March to early June 193.[5]

As for Genialis' brother-officer and correspondent Flavius Proculus, it cannot be excluded that he is the man of this name who received a rescript from the Emperor Hadrian: it laid down the conditions on which judgement was to be given. The case involved an appeal for freedom by a man alleged to be a slave belonging to the imperial treasury. This suggests that the Flavius Proculus involved was serving as a high-ranking magistrate or indeed provincial governor (*Digest* 49.14.3.9). But the names are very common, so this cannot be pressed.

At all events, Genialis and Proculus are the first of a group of men in the Vindolanda tablets whose family name was 'Flavius' – and there is also Hostilius Flavianus, a probable predecessor of Genialis, whose second name suggests that his mother was a Flavia. Before long, more Flavii appear in the tablets, also equestrian officers, Vindex and, most notably, Cerialis; and a correspondent of the latter was called Flavius Similis. Further, a Flavius [Ita]licus (or [Gal]licus) is referred to in a letter (1254); and yet another Flavius, who wrote to Priscinus, prefect of the First Tungrians, was Flavius Conianus (296). Of course, Flavius Gentilis is a reminder that some of these last three Flavii may have been, like him, freedmen. All the same, before the discovery of the Vindolanda tablets, hardly more than two equestrian officers with the name 'Flavius' marking them out as first or second generation Roman citizens, were known as early as AD 100, only four years after the fall of the Flavian dynasty.[6] All these Flavii, it may be added, may be assumed to have been called Titus, the *praenomen* shared by all three Flavian emperors and regularly adopted by those who took the name on acquiring Roman status. But *praenomina* were by now hardly used, even within the family, in most contexts, least of all by bearers of imperial names. What was the point, if all the Flavii were called Titus? *Praenomina* were mostly reserved for official documents – or for tombstones and other stone inscriptions.

Flavius Cerialis and his wife Sulpicia Lepidina

It has been suggested that Flavius Genialis could have gained his appointment directly from Trajan in AD 97 or 98, when the new Emperor was still in Lower Germany, and Flavius Cerialis might have been recommended to the governor of Britain, L. Neratius Marcellus, by Marcellus' brother Priscus, governor of Lower

Germany.[7] Governors of Britain had a great many posts to fill in the equestrian *militiae*, and were no doubt glad to have suitable men recommended. 'Suitable' meant, to be sure, in the case of those seeking their first commission, not much more than 'well educated, congenial persons' (or 'gentlemen'). Capacity to command soldiers and, not least, to run a regiment so that the men were fed and clothed, trained and disciplined, and their fort kept in good repair, was no doubt taken for granted. Potential officers mostly came from landowning families, and running an estate would give them all the experience necessary. For the rest, they could learn as they went along. Marcellus was approached by the Younger Pliny on behalf of his protégé, the young scholar Suetonius Tranquillus. Marcellus duly appointed him to be military tribune, but Suetonius then got cold feet and backed out of the appointment.[8] All the same, there is a faint chance that, even if Suetonius never arrived, some of his gear had been sent in advance to Britain and ended up being passed on to Cerialis (cf. below).

A man who certainly was one of Cerialis' brother-officers in northern Britain, Marcus Caecilius September, possibly owed his commission, and indeed, a previous one some years before, in Syria, to Pliny's patronage. The name September is exceedingly rare, being attested only once in all the European Latin-speaking parts of the empire other than at Rome, precisely at Pliny's home-town Comum – and Pliny had been born a Caecilius, so September could well have been his client. At any rate, Caecilius September, as prefect of a cohort in Syria in AD 88, served under the governor Valerius Patruinus, whose son-in-law, Domitius Apollinaris, was a friend of Pliny. Further, Neratius Marcellus was nephew by marriage of Patruinus, his wife Corellia Hispulla was related to Pliny's wife, and Marcellus later married Apollinaris' daughter as his second wife.[9]

Cerialis himself at one point tried his hand at a bit of patronage. Hearing that a fellow-officer called [G]rattius Crispinus was 'returning', he drafted a letter (225), obviously to be entrusted to Grattius, addressed to a high-ranking man also called Crispinus. [G]rattius, whose names strongly suggest that he came from the Saguntum area in eastern Spain, may, for example, have called in at Vindolanda at the end of his term of office as commander of another regiment. But he need not have been 'returning' either to Spain, to Rome or indeed anywhere outside Britain. He may perfectly well have been, for example, a legionary tribune who had been sent on a mission to the frontier zone and stayed at Vindolanda on his way back to his legionary base.

Cerialis obviously wanted to impress his high-ranking correspondent. This letter was not one to be dictated off the cuff. The language is certainly literary.[10] That he was taking special pains is also clear from several places where he had crossed words out and substituted others. The deletions are indicated below by double square brackets; words between single square brackets are suggestions to supply gaps in the text; those in round brackets are not in the Latin but are added to make the translation clearer:

> To his Crispinus.
> As [G]rattius Crispinus is returning [- - - -] [[I have not been for myself]]
> and [is coming?] to [you?], I have gladly embraced, Lord, the opportunity
> of greeting you – (who are) my Lord and (the man) for whom it is among

91 The start of Cerialis' draft letter to Crispinus (a fragment of 225)

my especial prayers [[to have]] that you may be in good health and fulfilling every one of [[his]] (your) hopes. For you have always deserved this from me, right up to this position of honour (? or rank/high office: the Latin word is restored as *d[ignita]tem*).

Relying on this, [?I ask] this of you first, [Lord?,- - - - that] you greet(?) the Right Honourable N[eratiu]s Marcellus, my Consular. By this means [you will gain?] the opportunity for yourself now to [enhance?] in his presence the fortunes of (your) friends, of whom I know that, [thanks to?] him, you have a great many. [?Therefore,] in whatever way you wish, fulfil whatever I await from you and set me up with very many (?) friends in such a way that by your favour I can enjoy a pleasant military service.

I write this to you from Vindolanda, [?in which place my] winter-quarters (*hiberna*) are.

One more, largely illegible line follows; there was no doubt a second sheet with at least a closing greeting.[11]

Cerialis presumably later dictated from this draft to an NCO with good hand-writing in his office, adding what is missing here, for example, at the beginning, *Flavius Cerialis* and *salutem*, and Crispinus' full names and rank on the back. The fair copy will then have been handed over to [G]rattius Crispinus to deliver to his namesake. Whoever he was, the recipient of the letter evidently had access to the governor, 'the Right Honourable man, my Consular', *v(irum) c(larissimum)*, *consularem meum*. *Vir claris-simus* was the standard title of rank for a member of the Senate, 'Consular', literally 'former consul', meant the governor of the province, whose official title was *legatus Augusti pro praetore*. The term 'consular' was used to distinguish him from the other legates in the province, the *legati legionum* and the *legatus iuridicus*, who were only ex-praetors. Cerialis' words, 'you have always deserved this of me right up to this position', suggest that he had known Crispinus for some time, at any rate since before he gained his present post, whatever that was. Perhaps they had met previously in Lower Germany? Crispinus could by this have been legate of one of the legions in Britain or the *iuridicus* of the province. It is possible that he was not a senator at all, but a high equestrian official, either the procurator or the prefect of the *classis Britannica*. But he was surely in Britain rather than, for example, at Rome, otherwise he could hardly have greeted Marcellus and have been 'in his presence'.[12]

Cerialis calls Vindolanda 'my winter-quarters', which might suggest that he was writing between late September and late March, and also implies that he was normally elsewhere in the campaigning season, which was certainly not the case. *Hiberna* was surely an old-fashioned usage, meaning a permanent fort rather than a temporary camp. What he was seeking to achieve by this letter is not entirely clear: 'fulfil whatever I await from you' is rather vague or indeed deliberately enigmatic. The odds are that Grattius had been briefed by Cerialis with further details, to be imparted to Crispinus verbally when he handed over the letter. On balance, it looks as if Cerialis hoped to gain commissions for some of his friends. It is true that the previous sentence gives the impression that Crispinus was being offered the opportunity, which Cerialis' request to greet Marcellus was to provide, to enhance the fortunes of *his own* friends. Cerialis was probably just being artful here. Perhaps he knew that there were, or soon would be, vacancies to command several neighbouring regiments and was trying his hand at nominating friends to fill them. The notion that he hoped to have friends serving in the vicinity – further recruits to the 'band of brothers' – makes perfect sense in the light of the evidence from the tablets: entertaining and visiting friends clearly formed an important part of Cerialis' life at Vindolanda.

Cerialis' *expensa*

The clearest insight into entertainment in the *praetorium* of Flavius Cerialis is given by eight pages of accounts, 111 lines in all, on five tablets, of which three are written on both sides. Cerialis himself is not named, but the consuls for AD 103 and 104 are registered, years which must belong to his period of office, and also, it may be argued, a consul of 102. Besides, three of the guests listed as lunching or dining are known from the letters as Cerialis' friends, brother-officers and correspondents – Brocchus, Niger and September. The original order of the sheets is not easy to establish, since the writer, probably a slave or freedman in Cerialis' household, seems to have been slightly slapdash. These can hardly be accounts kept on a day-to-day basis, but may represent a resumé written up later from notes or from memory. Further, about two fifths of each sheet is broken off on the right-hand side, so that many details are lost, including any sums of money that may have been entered, or incompletely preserved; and it is probable that at least one whole sheet which once existed is missing.[13]

What ought to be the first sheet – and if this is right, the year must be 101 – begins with an entry for 10 June. It registers *missio Flavi [ ]*, 'the send off of Flavius . . .': could this be a ceremony to mark the formal departure of Flavius Genialis, Cerialis' predecessor as prefect?[14] It was perhaps not long after this that Cerialis received a strange letter (256). The writer's name has been read as Flavius Genialis, but the lettering is rather faint: it could have been Genialis' freedman Gentilis.

92   Perhaps the first entries in Cerialis' expensa (Inv. 1474A.VI)

Whoever wrote the letter at any rate mentioned the other man on the first page, most of which is too fragmentary to give a clear sense. Then comes a curious statement: 'For if . . . to me, because I once did something mean to him, for this reason I have been up till now lingering in the thickets, to be safer there if you send him back.' 'Lingering in the thickets', *per silvolas repto*, literally 'I am crawling through the little woods', might mean 'going extra slowly, off the beaten track', 'keeping a low profile' or 'going into hiding'. 'To be safer there if you send him back': 'back to where?', one needs to know – to wherever the writer would otherwise have gone? Alas, the full story must remain a matter of guesswork unless another tablet turns up with more details.[15]

The next entry after the *missio* is for 30 August: 'at dinner, Niger and Brocchus'. These two must have commanded regiments not too far from Vindolanda; they wrote the joint letter (248) to Cerialis quoted in chapter 5, with the intriguing prediction that 'you will meet our Consular very soon'. That letter was perhaps sent not long before their visit: the closing greeting is followed by a PS, to be interpreted as 'expect us', *nos expec[ta]*. Niger need not be the Oppius Niger who wrote to Cerialis (249) and to a later Vindolanda prefect, Priscinus (295). The text of Oppius' letter to Cerialis is lost, but that to Priscinus shows that he was based at Bremetennacum (Ribchester), a long way south. The writer of the joint letter with Brocchus, who came to Vindolanda with him, could be Valerius Niger, who also wrote a letter to Vindolanda (465), although nothing of its contents has survived. Of course, Oppius Niger could have been transferred to Bremetennacum *c.*105, after being stationed previously somewhere close to Brocchus. The latter, by his full names C. Aelius Brocchus, was evidently stationed at a fort called Briga, probably on the Solway coast (see below, *Visiting Briga*). He was to become a close friend of Cerialis, and his wife Claudia Severa developed a very warm friendship with Cerialis' wife Sulpicia Lepidina.

Brocchus was a dinner guest in the next entry, for 25 December 101, and was back again on 17 January 102 – that is, if one may restore the entry in between as *k(alendis) Ianuaris Ser[viano ii cos.]*. This would register the year 102 by the abbreviated name of

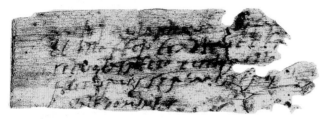

93 A strange letter to Cerialis (256)

the consul L. Julius Ursus Servianus. Two visits at this time of year: surely Brocchus came to join Cerialis on a hunt on each occasion. The two men's enthusiasm for hunting can be documented in several tablets (see below, *Hunting*). On 21 February there is reference to something coming 'from the poultry yard', *a stabulo*. On 1 March a religious festival was celebrated 'by the master', *dom[ino]* – or 'by the mistress', *dom[ina]*, Lepidina (or both, *dom[inis]*): it was the Matronalia, held annually on this day for the married women.

According to Roman tradition, it commemorated the founding of the temple of Juno Lucina, goddess of childbirth, on this day; Lucina was also a deity associated with the moon. The first of March had also originally marked the beginning of the Roman year. A late Roman commentator refers to men praying for the continuation of their marriage at the Matronalia. Christian accounts (hostile) tell of men wearing female clothing as part of the ceremonies. Basically, however, it was a women's festival, so that in the *praetorium* Lepidina surely had the major role. One may speculate that for an officer and his wife who probably both came from the Lower Rhineland, the Matronalia had an extra appeal: local goddesses called the *Matronae* or *Matres*, often with a great variety of different epithets of Celtic or Germanic origin, such as *Aufaniae* or *Octocannae*, were very widely worshipped there.[16]

On 11 April a distribution of beer to the decurions is registered, each receiving the same amount.[17] Coincidence or not, the next entry, for 16 May, also referred to beer: a *cervesar[ius]*, brewer, was there – replenishing the prefect's stocks? His name is missing; he may be the brewer Atrectus known from an account (182). Two days later another visit was connected with chickens, *pulli*, the first of numerous mentions of poultry. In some cases it is specifically stated that poultry was consumed. In others it is not clear whether poultry was being sold or being delivered. The former is perhaps more likely, in view of several entries referring to the 'poultry yard', *stabulum*. It may be inferred that the prefect kept chickens and

geese, principally to supply his own household
and his guests, but was prepared to sell birds to
his men.

The next line is slightly surprising: the fifth
consulship of Trajan, 103, is listed, but not in
conjunction with 1 January, as with the consular
dates for 102 and 104. One wonders if the
previous entries, covering only five weeks or so,
all referred to the previous year – perhaps the
writer forgot to put the consular date at the
beginning of this page and inserted it in the
middle. Be this as it may, the first entry definitely
of 103 is for 26 April, listing the presence of
Crescens, perhaps the centurion of that name;
and 'on the same day' someone else, name
missing, was there in connection with geese,
anseres. Only three more entries follow for AD
103, all from June: on the 5th a certain Suetius
was there, on the 10th a brewer called again, on
the 11th a man called Vatto is mentioned in
connection with chickens.

The account then jumps to the beginning of
the year 104, given by the consulship of Sextus
Attius Suburanus, its first entry, for New Year's
Day, registering a veteran, name missing, his
business 'chickens', then two members of the
regiment, Sautenus and Chnisso: in each case
something (missing) was received from them –
money for chickens, or chickens they supplied?
More chickens are registered on 2 January,
though no names are preserved. There follows

*94 Beer for the decurions (lines 2-
3) and Trajan's fifth consulship
(line 8) (Inv. 1474A.V)*

an entry for 1 March, when the Matronalia were probably celebrated again, and
a man perhaps named Pau[lus] was at the *praetorium*. On 30 and 31 March two
more men, Mar[inus?] and Exso[mnius?] were there, the latter perhaps the
centurion of this name. On 23 April a *iumentarius*, an ox- or mule-driver whose
name began with U- or V- is registered. After this entry there was a summing up
of how many geese, nursling chicks (*pulli adempti*) and chickens had changed
hands. For 30 April 'also nursling chicks' was entered, after which is an incomplete phrase, *per comm[. . .]*. This remains obscure: 'through trade', *per comm[ercium]*,
per comm[eatum], 'for provisions'? Another total of chickens or chicks, *summa
pul[lorum]*, concluded this sheet.

It is hard to be sure, because the right-hand side of the sheets is broken off,
whether the chickens and geese were being purchased by members of the garrison,
rather than supplied by them to the prefect. But one fragmentary account (1298B)

shows someone being charged for 21 chickens. Another (1299A) found next to it, evidently in the same handwriting, is headed 'account for 10 *denarii*', and concerns Chnisso, a soldier registered in the *praetorium expensa* on 1 January 102. The word *pulli* here is very faint, but it seems to be a bill for 'chickens with Chnisso': some (number too faint to read), 'for p(rivate?) use, *in usus p.*, 10 [or more] consumed, the remainder with Ch[nisso]'.

To return to the *expensa*, the remaining four pages are more informative, listing for the most part who ate what and when – and sometimes where. They seem to span the years 104-5, although no consular date for 105 is preserved, and are headed, after an illegible entry perhaps for 28 April, *expensa*. The next date is 18 May, assumed to be in 104: first a chicken is mentioned, perhaps in connection with lunch. 'On the same day' a visitor was 'dining', *cenan[te]* and another 'chicken was consumed', *absumptus*. A single chicken was eaten on 25 May, when someone whose name ended –ius was a guest. For 13 June is registered *c[enante? . . .] legati*: as dinner guest a staff-member (?) 'of the legate'. This would be the legate of a legion – the governor was the 'Consular' – and probably that based at Eburacum, IX Hispana. Then on 14 June, Cerialis (it may be assumed, though he is not named) was *Coris iussu [ ]*, 'at Coria, on the orders' of someone, perhaps of the legate. 'On the same day' a number of '[chickens?] perished in [the poultry-yard?]' – to give the likely restoration. (One cannot imagine this document listing deaths of soldiers in battle.)

A sheet written on both sides may be missing at this point. At any rate, on what appears to be the next one, the first entry is for 15 March, presumably of 105. Niger was again a dinner-guest, this time with a different colleague, whose name is fragmentary and faint, perhaps Pastor (known as a correspondent and fellow-officer of Cerialis, 259). The entry for 21 March may be connected with a festival for the goddess Minerva – only *[ ]vae* is preserved, but the day was regularly celebrated as her birthday. On 4 April Brocchus was a visitor again, on the 29th two more colleagues came to lunch, one being (Caecilius) September; the other guest's name is lost.

In May Sautenus, who seems to have been on Cerialis' staff – perhaps his poul-tryman – is mentioned three times. 'At Sautenus' (quarters)', *apud Sautenum*, is regis-tered as the venue of a meal on 4 May. This is followed by a summary of expenses, and a listing of how many geese (and probably chickens as well) were still available. On 9 May there was some ceremony *ad sig[na]*, 'at the standards', involving a man called Onesimus: this was conceivably the ancient roses-festival, known to have been celebrated in the Roman army at this time of year, as the *rosalia signorum*.[18] Onesimus may have been the regimental standard-bearer; if so, he was a Batavian soldier with a Greek name. 'On the same day, Sautenus' is mentioned again, this time 'in the poultry-yard', *in stabuló*, but what was involved is lost in the gap. On 29 May guests came to lunch: the name of the first is missing, the other was called Flavinus. He cannot be identified with certainty, but the name, not all that common, was espe-cially popular in Spain.[19] He might well have been a brother-officer of Spanish origin. 'On the same day' something took place *apud Sautenum* again.

95 Chickens at the praetorium AD 103-4 (line 7 gives the consulship of Sextus Attius Suburanus: Inv. 1474A.II)

96   *The arrival of the Consular, AD 105? (1474A.I: the great man's visit is registered five lines from the bottom)*

The next entry marked a major occasion, 'the arrival of the governor', *adventu consu[laris]*. Irritatingly, the date is given as 'the Kalends of May', 1 May, although as it follows an entry for the end of May it is probably a mistake for 1 June. At any rate, a number of items (chickens? geese? something finer?) 'were consumed at lunch', *in prandio absu[mpti]*, then comes 'and likewise at Coria . . .', *item Coris m . . . .[ ]*. Cerialis evidently then accompanied the governor to Coria. It is a pity that the governor's name is not given. Neratius Marcellus, named by Cerialis in his draft letter to Crispinus, and probably the man who had given Cerialis his commission, was probably no longer in office by 105. His successor is not known. It might have been Lucius Publilius Celsus.[20] Visits by the governor were presumably a normal occurrence at least once during his term of office, if not annually, when he inspected the forts. If the chronology of these *expensa* here put forward is right, a visit by the governor in early summer 105 is particularly significant. He may have arrived with important orders to the Batavians and other regiments: start preparing to leave Britain. Vindolanda was not to be abandoned, as other forts were, notably those in Scotland. But it was a major moment in the history of the frontier.

The last entry on the penultimate page of the *expensa*, for 6 June, simply registers that someone whose name is missing delivered or bought four chickens. The final sheet only has one date, 16 July, followed by 'through Surenus', perhaps with the symbol 7 for centurion after his name, and 'capons (?)[or black grouse (?)], 12 in number', *[capo]nes* (or *[tetrao]nes*) *n xii [ ]*. 'On the same day' a man perhaps called P[ater]nus is mentioned in connection with chickens and Sautenus crops up yet again. This time he was apparently in charge of something which was *penes Sautenum*. It could have been a party for the prefect's personal guardsmen, *[singula]ribus*. The accounts end with summaries of poultry consumption. Soon afterwards the Ninth Batavians were ready to leave. These sheets, along with a good many other writing tablets and other 'rubbish' were piled up outside the *praetorium* on the intervallum road and set on fire. Fortunately it must have rained heavily before they had all burned.

Visiting Briga

The *expensa* alone would give more insight into activity in a *praetorium* than is available for any other Roman fort at this time. There are some other records of a similar type as well. A document of some 40 lines (190) registers consumption of barley, beer, wine and vinegar, pork-fat and fish-sauce over seven days, between 19 and 25 June, in an unknown year. In one case the wine is apparently described as 'Massic', a highly prized variety from Campania. On 24 June the 'Lord', *dominus*, 'through Privatus', *per Privatum*, probably his slave, donated a *modius* of wine for 'the festival of the goddess', *sacrum d(i)vae*. This unnamed deity was no doubt Fors Fortuna, goddess of Fortune, whose festival was regularly celebrated on that day each year. Cerialis himself was evidently not in residence: the account ends with the entry 'the *domini* [presumably meaning the Lord and his Lady, *dominus* and the *domina*] have remained at Briga', *domini Brigae man[se]runt*.

It is not hard to guess what Cerialis and Lepidina were doing at Briga, staying there as guests of their friends Aelius Brocchus and Claudia Severa. That this couple was based at Briga is strongly suggested by a letter from Severa to Lepidina (292):

> I, sister, just as I had spoken with you, and promised that I would ask Brocchus, and that I would come to you – I did ask him, and he replied that it is always, wholeheartedly, permitted to me, together with . . . to come to you in whatsoever way I can. There are, truly, certain intimate matters which [I long to discuss with you (?). As soon as I know for sure (?),] you will receive my letter, from which you will know what I am going to do . . . I was . . . and I will remain at Briga. Farewell, my dearest sister and my most longed for soul. To Sulpicia Lepidina from Severa, wife of Brocchus.

'I will remain at Briga' surely means that Severa and Brocchus were living at this place. Severa's letter must have been written after the two young women – probably still in their teens – had already met and become close friends. Brocchus, on one of his visits to Vindolanda in 101 or 102, could well have invited Cerialis to bring Lepidina to stay at Briga. That could be the visit in June mentioned above. Less than three months later, if it was in the same year, Severa invited Lepidina to visit her for a special occasion (291):

> On 11 September, sister, for the celebration of my birthday, I ask you warmly to come to us, you will make the day more enjoyable by your presence. Greet your Cerialis. My Aelius and our little son greet you. Farewell, sister, dearest soul, as I hope to prosper, and hail.

97   Severa hopes to visit Lepidina (292)

98   Lepidina is invited to Severa's birthday party (291)

The script of the main body of Severa's letters shows that they were dictated to a scribe in Brocchus' office, but that the last sentence, with the very tender greeting, was added in Severa's own, unpractised hand. This was also the case with a third letter from her to Lepidina (293), of which only part of the closing greeting, 'Farewell . . . dearest sister', is preserved. On one occasion when Lepidina had travelled somewhere without her husband, perhaps to this birthday party, Cerialis evidently asked Clodius Super to escort her on her way back. Super had been unable to do this, to judge from the opening of his letter (1498+1500): 'I would gladly have met Lepidina on her way back, as you wished, brother . . . '

The name Briga is apparently not recorded elsewhere. Still, there is a possibility that it is listed, as *Bribra*, in the *Ravenna Cosmography*, a work compiled centuries later, *c.*700. Scores of names in the British section are seriously misspelt, and the emendation from 'Bribra' to 'Briga' is less extreme than required for many other places. 'Bribra' is listed between 'Alauna' and 'Maio', generally identified with Maryport and Bowness-on-Solway respectively. An attractive location in this area would be Kirkbride, where a fort of the right period has been identified. Pottery found there is all datable to the years 80-120. The Coria-Luguvalium road – the Stanegate – can be regarded as having extended beyond Luguvalium, as far as Kirkbride. 'Kirkbride' means 'the church of (St) Bride', another form of Brigit, and an ancient place-name Briga could very easily have been interpreted in early Christian times as Brigit. 'Briga' means 'high' or 'hill' in old Celtic and although Kirkbride is on the Solway Plain, the fort was at the highest point of a low ridge.[21] If this identification is correct, a stay at Briga would have given Cerialis and Lepidina an attractive change of scene, with dramatic views of the Lakeland hills, Skiddaw and Saddleback, to the south, of the Solway Firth – *Ituna*, the name of the River Eden which flows into it, to the Romans – and of Criffel, Nithsdale and Annandale, home of the

Anavionenses, to the west. The distance involved in a journey from Vindolanda, some 70km, could probably have been covered in two days journey on horseback, with stops for refreshment and one overnight stay possible from a choice of four Stanegate forts (Carvoran, Nether Denton, Brampton Old Church and Luguvalium) on the way there and back.

Kirkbride must have been an important communications and supply base. There was still easy access to the sea there in Roman times. It was at the tidal limit of the River Wampool, which flows into the protected inlet now called 'Moricambe', and surely controlled a harbour. ('Moricambe' – 'curved bay' – was actually applied in Ptolemy's *Geography* to Morecambe Bay, which was only so renamed in 1771.)[22] Not only Roman ships would have put in there, bringing supplies from the south to the northern forts. No doubt traders from Ireland visited too. A fine wooden beaker found at Vindolanda was made of Irish yew – the people of Iron Age Ireland made no pottery, but their skills at metalworking and wood-carving were remarkable.

We have already seen Brocchus as a visitor at Vindolanda on three occasions between late August 101 and February 102, and once more in early April 105. Besides this, Cerialis and Brocchus were together on one occasion with someone called Celsus – when their activities involved hunting (1453). Celsus might conceivably have been the successor of Neratius Marcellus as governor.[23] Yet a likelier identification is another brother-officer, Gaius Valerius Celsus, prefect of a cavalry regiment, the *ala Pannoniorum Tampiana*. Although nothing is known about where the *ala* was stationed, Valerius Celsus is known to have been its prefect on 19 January 103. This information comes from a diploma found at Malpas in Cheshire, issued to a decurion of the regiment, a man from Spain, not Pannonia where the regiment had been raised. (Unlike the Batavians and Tungrians, other auxiliary regiments were no longer drawing recruits from the original territory.) This is also the document that dates Neratius Marcellus' gover-norship – he had undoubtedly arrived before 103, probably in 101. Further, it is also the earliest unequivocal evidence for the First Tungrians being a double-cohort, *milliaria*.[24]

A letter from Brocchus to Cerialis (1503A) – the only one of his from which enough survives to work out the subject – written just after the Saturnalia, which began on 17 December and lasted for three days, seems to end with an invitation for Cerialis and Lepidina to spend the New Year's holiday with him and Severa: 'come with Lepidina, just as . . . at the Kalends', *c[um] Lepidina veni sicu[t . . .]apud Kalendas.* Brocchus can be seen to have helped Cerialis out in several ways. There is a draft letter to him (233) in which Cerialis begins: 'If you love me, brother, I ask that you send me hunting-nets' and adds that 'you should repair the pieces very strongly.' This was by no means all that Brocchus provided. A 'clothing list' (196) found in the Period III *praetorium* includes a number of items for dinner-wear, some of them 'from Tranquillus', others 'from Brocchus'. They were certainly sent for Cerialis to wear.

This list, of which only part survives, is worth quoting:

. . . for dining.

(One or more) pair(s) of blankets.

White (?) capes, *paenulae*, . . .

From an outfit, *synthesi*:

capes . . . and a cloak, *laena*, and a [tunic?]

for dining.

A *sunthesi[na]* (a word meaning 'garment').

A scarf (or scarves) (?), *subpaenu[la(s)]* (the meaning of this word is not quite certain)

. . .

Vests . . .

from Tranquillus.

A scarf (or scarves)

from Tranquillus' – this line is crossed out and below is written

'From Brocchus,

tunics, . . .

. . . half-belted

tunics, for dining (?), *cen[atorias?]*.

On the back of the tablet various other items are entered, in a different hand, including a vase with a handle and some rings. It is not clear whether they refer to the same consignment. As far as the clothing is concerned, Cerialis was evidently being kitted out with items of the kind an equestrian officer was expected to wear. Had Brocchus noticed that his friend was not properly dressed? Of course, it might be that Tranquillus and Brocchus simply forwarded items which Cerialis had ordered, which had been sent by ship to Briga. Tranquillus must be assumed to have been another brother-officer, but the name was far from common – less than 20 examples are known. A famous bearer of it was the scholar Suetonius Tranquillus, the future biographer of the Caesars. It is a curious coincidence that the Younger Pliny had obtained him a tribunate from Neratius Marcellus, obviously in the army of Britain. Suetonius had second thoughts and asked for the commission to be transferred to a kinsman, Caesennius Silvanus. Pliny duly arranged this.[25] Is it possible that Suetonius had had a box of his gear, including blankets, dining outfits and vests sent ahead to Britain, sold or made available to Cerialis when its owner backed out of his commission?

None of these pieces of clothing were intended for Lepidina, it seems, and her clothing is not identifiable among the numerous textile fragments uncovered from her husband's *praetorium*. All that can be inferred is that the clothing worn by its occupants was predominantly of diamond twill. Some of the textiles were once brightly coloured and there was some decoration: traces of what was probably purple can be detected, also 'a tapestry-woven notched gamma symbol' inserted into a piece of fine half-basket weave.[26] Cerialis, it may be guessed, was the owner of a high status shoe with 'fishnet' openwork upper. For the design to be effective, it is suggested, he must have worn brightly coloured socks. It is pretty well certain that a group of four narrow, elegantly

99   New kit for Cerialis (196)

proportioned ladies' shoes, all *c.*21/22cm in length, size 32/33, belonged to Lepidina. Only the soles survive in three cases, two being stitched, from light outdoor shoes for summer wear, the others being nailed, one with the impression of her foot still visible, the other with the well-worn upper still attached. Best of all, the elegant lady's sandal, size 33, decorated with rosettes and stamped on the sole with the maker's name, L. Aeb(utius) Thales, surely belonged to her as well.[27] It is, further, probable that what was at first thought to have been an unfinished basket was headgear worn by Lepidina to keep off insects. It is woven from the cleaned cores of hair moss stems, woven to form a round cap about 17cm wide, from the edge of which bare strands project as a fringe.[28]

100 Shoes from Cerialis' praetorium: the largest is probably one of his own

Officers' children

The 'little son', *filiolus*, of Brocchus and Severa, is mentioned in two letters (292, 1329).[29] That Cerialis and Lepidina also had one or more children, who were with them at Vindolanda, can be inferred partly from the children's shoes found in the *praetorium*, the sizes of which range between 17 and 23, suitable for children aged between two and ten years old – since Cerialis and Lepidina spent some four years at Vindolanda, the various sizes may reflect the presence of only one or two growing boys. A child's sock, made from two separate pieces of woollen twill, roughly tacked together, *c*.16cm x 7cm, and an insole for a child's shoe, neatly cut from an old piece of fine compact diamond twill, almost the same size (but 0.5cm longer) was also found in a Period III level.[30] There is less certainty about 'your boys', *pueros tuos*, greeted by Cerialis' colleague Justinus (260). This might mean 'your sons', but it is more likely that Justinus was referring to Cerialis' household slaves or perhaps (parallels are lacking) to his soldiers.

Another, quite different piece of evidence for a child is the tablet (118) with a single line – not even a complete sentence – from the great Roman classic, Virgil's *Aeneid*, IX 473. It is rather clumsily written, in 'rustic' capital letters, on the back of a draft letter: *interea pavidam volitans pinnata p' vbem*, 'meanwhile, the winged (bird – meaning the personified 'Rumour'), flying through the trembling city'. The second last word is rendered in abbreviated form, *p'* instead of *per*, and the last one misspelled *ubem* instead of *urbem*. This is followed by *segn.*, in 'normal' handwriting. There seems no doubt that it is a writing-exercise by a small boy. *Segn* probably represents the comment, *segn(iter)*, 'slack', by a tutor, a slave or freedman in Cerialis' household. Apart from Privatus, named in the account cited above (190), Cerialis had at least one other slave with him, Primigenius, recipient of a letter (347) from a fellow-slave called Rhenus. Further possible evidence of a son comes from another tablet (121) with a drawing, or rather a doodle, and a few

*101 Lepidina's smart
slipper*

*102 Lepidina's anti-
insect headpiece*

*103 A child's sock from
the* praetorium

104 *A letter from Justinus to*
     Cerialis (260)

105   A not very good piece of homework (118): a line from the Aeneid *(IX 473)*

letters possibly attempting the words *belli regna*. That could be an echo of another
Virgilian line, *Aeneid* XII 567: *causam belli regna ipsa Latini*, 'the cause of the war,
the kingdom of Latinus'. At all events, there was at least one copy of a classical
Latin work in the prefect's house.

It is striking that it was the last books of the great Roman epic that were being
read at Vindolanda. The favourite ones for most readers (and for graffiti) were II,
on the capture of Troy and Aeneas' escape, IV, on his romance with Dido, and VI,
his visit to the Underworld. The last six books, covering the Trojans' battles against
the Latins may have had more appeal for the Romanised Batavians. In book VIII
there is the stirring account of the battle of Actium, as shown on the shield of
Aeneas, 626-731, where even the Batavians' homeland, the Rhine island, gets a
kind of mention at the end, 727, *Rhenusque bicornis*. The long account of the origin
of the Roman festival of Hercules in this book (185-279) would have gone down
well with worshippers of Magusanus Hercules, it may be imagined. The line from
book IX copied in Cerialis' *praetorium* looks harmless enough, with the metaphor
of 'Rumour' flying like a bird over a anxious (besieged) city. But it is immediately
preceded by the bloodbath in the camp of the Rutulians – and 'Rumour' was
bringing Euryalus' mother the news of her son's awful death. Still, the prefect's son,
like other small boys, probably enjoyed this sort of thing. Cerialis himself would
certainly have had a full dose of Virgil in his own boyhood – and probably of
Sallust, Ovid and other classics as well. A fragment of a Period III letter (333)
actually mentions books, so perhaps Cerialis and Lepidina had their own reading
matter. It would be nice to imagine that they were sent early copies of two recent
monographs of which the subjects should have appealed strongly to a prefect of
Batavians stationed in Britain, Tacitus' *Agricola* and *Germany* (Pliny's *Panegyric* of
Trajan, delivered in 100, would have been rather too long and heavy going). There
were some contemporary poets as well: Statius, who had just finished producing,
but was probably dead, Martial, who went on for several years more, and Juvenal,
just starting to publish. Perhaps Vindolanda will one day yield up from the depths
a line or two from one of these authors.

A draft letter (227) may give a further clue to Cerialis having a son: it is headed
'Flavius Cerialis', but this has been crossed out, and the name of the intended
recipient has not been written. The brief text begins with a reference to the
'birthday of my Cerialis', *natalem Cerialis mei*; *natalem* has also been crossed out

*106 A small boy's doodle
     during a lesson
     (121)?*

and replaced by *valetudinem*, 'health' – or 'ill-health' – followed by 'for I want you [*vobis*, plural, crossed out and replaced by *te*, singular] to be clear about my intentions'. It may be that Cerialis was composing an excuse for not being able to accept an invitation, giving first his son's birthday – in which case his son was also called Cerialis – as the reason, then substituting his ill-health. But it could equally well be that after Cerialis had begun the letter, he decided to ask Lepidina to write – or dictate – the text, and that first the birthday, then the ill-health, of Cerialis himself was her idea.

Slaves

As for the rest of the household, it is plausible that Lepidina had her own, female slaves. A letter to her from a woman perhaps called Paterna (294) can be read to mean that she was being given one or two new ones: 'So may I be in good health, Lady, that I shall bring you two slave-girls (?), one . . . , the other free from fever (?) . . . '. Another letter (1309), probably written by a female slave to a fellow slave-woman in the prefect's household, is unfortunately too fragmentary to assign with certainty to Lepidina's occupancy. But it also mentions 'two girls'. What survives begins with a reference to 'the Lady', then the writer insists that 'you should take care that he who reads out my letter to you should not inform the Lady of anything different'. It ends with greetings for a person, probably male, whose name ended *-ides*, and for 'our two girls', followed by 'Farewell, sister'. Another woman, called Valatta, wrote a letter to Cerialis (257) begging a favour: 'I ask, my Lord, by your descendants and by Lepidina, to grant me what [I request].'[31] Perhaps she was a slave belonging to Cerialis – for example, a former wet-nurse – writing from home, and requesting that she be granted her freedom.

Other slaves of Cerialis have already been mentioned. Another letter (1543+1548) was perhaps written by Cerialis to a member of his household staff when he was away from Vindolanda, for example at Coria. It shows concern that if friends arrived in his absence they should be welcomed and looked after: 'You should all make sure that if any friends should have come they are well received . . . ' Mention is made of 'two chickens' and 'wine', then that 'after the lunch guests have been sent on their way, you should hurry to Coria in the four-wheeler'. A fragment of a letter to Cerialis (1246) suggests that a friend coming from some distance was in need of advice on where to stay en route: '. . . order that . . . be given – and a lodging, where the nags (*caballi*) are handsome. Farewell, my dearest brother.' Another friend wrote thanking someone at Vindolanda, perhaps Cerialis again, 'that we are able, thanks to your generosity, to celebrate the festival more elegantly' (1281). One fragmentary letter (1310), not definitely to Cerialis, shows generosity being abused by someone: 'you know that he is (often?) drunk . . . and kindnesses are ruined by envy'.

Correspondence with friends

A draft of a letter from Cerialis to his friend and colleague Caecilius September (234) shows Cerialis doing September a service: 'Tomorrow, that is on 5 October, as you wish, Lord, I will make the goods ready'. The letter goes on with a reference to the weather: 'so that we may endure the storms, even if they are troublesome'. This text contains clear evidence that on this occasion the letter was dictated: the scribe, having heard the word 'storms', *tempestates*, misheard what followed as 'and winter', *et hiem* – *h* was no longer sounded in spoken Latin. It had to be crossed out and replaced by *etiam si*, 'even if'. Slightly more informative, if only for the closing greeting, is what remains of a letter to Cerialis from his colleague Justinus (260), possibly the same man as Claudius Justi[nus], who wrote another letter (1408B) to Vindolanda. Justinus wrote: 'With great pleasure I bring to your notice that [maddeningly, this news is missing] . . . I pray, Lord brother, that you may be very happy and in good health. Greet from me our Vindex and your boys.' 'Your boys' might have been Cerialis' sons, but more probably Justinus meant 'your slaves' or perhaps 'your soldiers'. As for 'our Vindex', the name is very common. It occurs again three times in the tablets, once in a letter to Cerialis (1443) from a man called Ingenuus, who seems to have been at Vinovia (Binchester) and in another fragment referring to the punishment of a serious offender (1340, cf. chapter 3); and a Flavius Vindex wrote to someone at Vindolanda (1477B). The latter, at least, may have been a fellow-officer. 'Our Vindex', seemingly at Vindolanda, may have been, for example, an NCO on Cerialis' staff, whom Justinus knew.

Most of Cerialis' remaining draft letters, apart from those already mentioned, have little more than his name at the top preserved (e.g. 237, 240, 241). Another (235) at least has the name of his correspondent, Similis, probably the Flavius Similis whose name and the beginning of that of Cerialis – and nothing else – are preserved in a fragment (254), and again as the writer of another, of which the recipient's name as well the contents are lost (286). Finally, a man called Similis was the owner of the slave Rhenus who wrote (347) to Cerialis' slave Primigenius. Similis might have been a fellow-officer serving somewhere not far away, but it is not impossible that he was a kinsman of Cerialis, for example a younger brother, who was back at home, in the Batavian country. The name Rhenus, 'Rhine', is at least a hint of this. A further fragment of a draft worth mentioning (236) shows Cerialis writing to a fellow-officer: it opens 'On the third day before the Kalends, brother, I have been waiting until the . . . hour . . . ' But whether he was waiting for some message concerned with military affairs or merely a social visit is, alas, unknown.

Hunting

Cerialis was a passionate hunter. In a draft letter (233) to his friend Brocchus he wrote, 'if you love me, brother, send me hunting-nets' (*plagae*). He adds on the second sheet that 'you should repair the pieces very strongly'. Such nets could be over 9m long and were spread across places where game was known to live. Brocchus clearly shared this passion: he was later to dedicate an altar in Pannonia to Diana, the goddess of hunting.[32] Cerialis refers to 'my huntsmen', *venatores mei*, in a draft letter to another correspondent (1453), and Brocchus is mentioned there too, as 'having returned from Ce[l]sus (?) after I did. I think that he, with many [huntsmen?] . . . ' Cerialis' huntsmen recall the Elder Pliny on geese (*NH* 10. 52ff.), not only bred for the table, he writes – including the specially fattened liver, *foie gras* – but, especially the white ones in Germany, prized 'for their feathers, which fetch five *denarii* a pound. This results in prefects of auxiliary regiments getting into trouble for sending whole cohorts away from outpost duty to capture these birds.' Pliny also mentions 'the most sumptuous feast that Britain knows, the barnacle-goose (*chenerotes*.'.

In the case of Cerialis and Brocchus, one feels that they hunted for the love of it, not to make a profit from goose-feathers. Horace's famous poem on country life (*Epodes* 2, *beatus ille qui procul negotiis*) sings of the joys of the winter hunt: driving fierce boars into the waiting *plagae*, stretching out the *retia* to snare the greedy thrushes, catching the timid hare and the crane with a *laqueus*. By the time of Trajan and Hadrian, the hare was hunted with dogs rather than snared. Cerialis' predecessors clearly hunted too. Genialis seems to have kept hunting-dogs. Surviving fragments of a writing tablet (1475) that probably derives from Genialis' term of office include a good many names – including 'Genialis', perhaps the prefect himself – and also what

107 'If you love me brother' (233)

are surely the names for two breeds, *segosi* and *vertrag(u)m*. The fullest account of them is in the treatise on hunting, *Cynegetica*, by Arrian (Flavius Arrianus). His career culminated in the governorship of Cappadocia in the 130s, so that the *Cynegetica* was written at most a few decades after Genialis and Cerialis were at Vindolanda.

Arrian is the only ancient writer to name and describe the first breed. He writes (*Cyneg.* 3:)

> . . . that kind of dog is no less skilled . . . at scenting animal tracks. But in appearance they are unattractive and wild. They bark or howl on the trail, like Carian hounds, but even more uncontrollably, when they have found the scent. Sometimes they are still over-excited the next day . . . But for tracking down and pursuing the hare when it has started to move they are not inferior to the Carian or to the Cretan hounds – except for speed . . . These dogs are called *Segousiai* [the female form], getting their name from a Celtic people, which, so I believe, was the first to breed and value them . . . As to their appearance, it is only worth mentioning that they are shaggy and ugly, the purer the breed the uglier. Among the Celts there is a famous comparison of these dogs with roadside beggars, because of their mournful and miserable voice and because they follow their prey not with a keen sound but with importunate and pitiful howls.'

Although this is the solitary ancient reference to *Sego(u)si*, they are referred to several times in the early Germanic law codes (which lay down penalties for stealing them).[33]

Vertragi are mentioned by several classical authors. Martial, writing at about the time of this tablet, describes (14. 200) how 'the keen *vertragus* brings the hare, undamaged by its teeth, to its master'. The name, variously written in ancient times, also occurs in the Germanic law-codes, as *veltravi*. Arrian, who himself had a much-loved *vertragus* bitch called *Hormé* ('Eagerness'), supplies the fullest description:

> The really fast Celtic dogs are called *vertragoi* in the Celtic language, not from the name of a people . . . , but because of their speed. There is nothing finer to look at than the shape and appearance of the best bred of these dogs,

108 Hunting dogs: a greyhound, vertrag(u)m, (left-hand side) and segosi (right-hand side) (fragments of Inv. 1475A)

whether you look at their eyes or their whole body or their coat or their colour. The variety of colour on the dappled variety is remarkable, while the plain-coloured ones seem to shine and are a very fine spectacle for the hunter. First of all they are long from head to tail, and there is no other sign of speed and good breeding in any breed of dog which is so important for speed as length (by contrast short ones are slow and badly bred).

More detail follows, on the best length of body, size and shape of head, eyes, 'large, high up, bright and shining, so as to dazzle one who looks at them', ears which should be 'should be large and soft, the neck long, round and flexible, which prevents them from damaging themselves when straining at the leash' and so on. 'They should have a broad chest, shoulder blades set apart . . . the legs long, straight and compact, the ribs strong, the back broad and firm, not fleshy but with good muscles, flanks hollow, the tail light, long, hairy and flexible . . . as it is difficult for them on a slope not to be outrun by the hare, it seems to me preferable when the hindlegs are longer than the forelegs.' He advises on feeding: 'Some dogs eat greedily, others modestly. The latter is a sign of better breeding. Good hounds . . . prefer bread and barley-cake. This is best for them . . . best of all is if they like dry food. . . . In winter food should be given once a day, shortly before dusk . . . In summer it is no bad thing to give them some bread during the day . . . and an egg in hot weather.' Arrian even adds that 'they like nothing better than a soft, warm bed. It is best when they sleep with a man.'[34]

Genialis or a previous prefect may have acquired the hounds. They were clearly still there under Cerialis. A writing tablet from his *praetorium* (1478) found on the 'bonfire' lists 'dogs' collars', *collares kanum*, among miscellaneous items that had been repaired, and there are numerous paw-prints on tiles from the bath-house. Cerialis must have hunted deer: a detailed account (191) of food and drink consumed by his household includes roe-deer (*capream*) and venison (*cervinam*). This is nicely confirmed by study of the animal-bones found at Vindolanda, which indicates a far greater proportion of deer than at other Roman sites.[35] Another document (1462) from the 'bonfire' site lists hunting gear, categorised as 'nets', *retes*, 'that we have left behind' – meaning, no doubt, when the Batavians went off to the Second Dacian War. The list reveals that Cerialis went after birds of all sizes: one net was for catching thrushes, *retem turdarem*, one was for duck, *anatarem*, and there were also three snares (or lassoes?) for catching swans, *laquii cicnares*. Seven further *laquii*, which would probably be made of deer-sinew, were left with a veteran. A fishing-net, *evericlum piscatorium*, is also listed. Fishing in the Chineley burn below the fort, in the River South Tyne and in the small lakes (called 'loughs') north of Vindolanda, Grindon, Crag Lough, Greenlee and Broomlee, no doubt produced salmon, trout and pike. A letter (271), probably to Cerialis, appears to thank him for sending something, and mentions *apuas*, a word meaning 'small fish'.

The idea of eating thrushes, or fieldfares, may be abhorrent to modern Britons. Romans ate them with relish. Varro (*RR* 3.2.15) claimed to know a breeder who sold 5000 at three *denarii* apiece. Horace (*Epist.* 1.15.41) portrays a greedy fellow saying 'There's nothing better than a fat thrush!'

109   Hunting-nets that were left behind (Inv. 1462)

One clue to where Vindolanda prefects went stag-hunting is supplied by a relief of the goddess Diana from Crow Hall Farm, close to the River South Tyne, less than 3km south-east of the fort. The stone might have belonged to a rural shrine, but could have been moved in post-Roman times from Vindolanda. It seems certain that there was a temple to a hunting deity at Vindolanda itself, probably Diana. An altar, decorated with carvings of a running stag and two fawns grazing in a wood, was found there in the eighteenth century, together with large quantities of stags' horns and pilasters and Doric capitals. Part of a relief of the goddess (the head is missing), of local buff sandstone, was found in 1999, reused as flooring for a late building just inside the south-west corner of the stone fort. She stands with right hand extended towards a torch, her left holding a bow. A graceful hound sits at her feet, looking towards her with upturned snout. [36]

Lepidina's kitchen

An insight into the kitchen in the *praetorium* is given by two fragments of what looks like an inventory (194) of its contents.[37] The first reads:

> shallow dishes (*scutulas*), 2
> side-plates (*paropsides*), 5
> vinegar-bowls (*acetabula*), 3
> egg-cups or egg-containers (*ovaria*), 3
> on the cross-beam:
> a platter (*lancem*), a shallow dish'

The second lists:

> 'a container (*compendiarium*) and
> a bronze lamp (*lucern[am] aeneam*)
> bread-baskets (*panaria*), 4(?)
> cups (*calices*), 2
> in a box (*the[ca]*), bowls or ladles (*trullas*), 2.'

Items of food that had been ordered (*mandat[a]*), probably for use in the *praetorium*, are listed in a fragmentary account (204): they include beans (?), lentils, lovage, starch, and butter. Fragments of what looks like a recipe (208) survive: it seems to have involved something made 'in the Batavian fashion', and included garlic paste (*alliatum*) and probably a spicy flavouring (*condit[um]*). A long list (191) of food of various kinds shows that chicken and geese were by no means all that was consumed in the *praetorium*: it includes spices, roe-deer, salt, young pig, ham, wheat, red deer.

A good deal certainly had to be ordered from far afield. A fragmentary account (1503B) registers items 'ordered (*mandata*) through Adiutor from London'. These include a *contrullium cenatorium*, which must be 'a set of bowls for dining' – although the first word is previously unattested – costing 11 *denarii*, mustard, anise, caraway

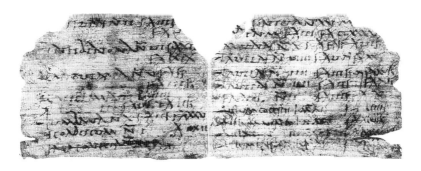

110   An invoice for an expensive delivery (Inv. 1398)

and thyme. Another account (1350) is quite miscellaneous: foodstuffs predominate, but other items occur too, in no obvious order. The right-hand side is missing, so that the quantities involved and their prices are missing: 'iron, . . . pounds; bitumen; bull's glue; pitch, . . . pounds, blacking, . . . pounds; ox-tongue (*anchusa*, a plant used for cosmetic purposes); mustard, . . . pounds; verdigris, . . . pounds; (an uncertain quantity of) honey-cloth (*lini mellari* – presumably used for sieving the beeswax from honey-combs); resin; cummin; oak-gall; anise; nuts; grapes; wheat; beans; potash.'

A much more detailed list (1398), this time not including anything edible, lists very precisely what each item cost. It begins with two locks, followed by six cloaks with buckles, five headbands, nine pounds of hair, ten underpants (or loin-cloths, *lumbaria*), a saddle (*scordiscus*), 15 cloaks made of bark (?), ten bags, three sets of skillets, each clearly a different kind, for they were priced differently, two sets of reins, and finally curtains, one scarlet, one green, two purple and one yellow. The most expensive single item was the curtains, costing respectively 54.5, 46.5, over 44 and over 55 *denarii*, while the nine pounds of hair cost nearly 52 *denarii* and the saddle – or leather horse-cloth – 12.

In a very fragmentary account (1467), only one word is clearly legible: *opium*. According to the Elder Pliny (20. 198ff.), dried poppy juice was indeed used as a soporific and for a variety of medical purposes – but he warns that an overdose could be fatal. Two documents are labelled 'Gavo's account' (*ratio Gavonis*) and list items which this man, mentioned in a letter to Flavius Genialis quoted above, supplied. The first (192) included a coverlet, 55 *modii* of beans, 38 pounds of wool, three bedspreads, honey, and a thick cloak (*sagum*). The other (207) begins with items supplied by Gavvo (as his name is spelled in the list itself) but ends with those 'from Marcus'. They all seem to be various types of clothing: several kinds of cloak, tunics and capes.

Priscinus

The *praetorium* of Period III was replaced by a barrack in Period IV, and the prefects of the First Tungrians had their residence elsewhere. Hence far fewer tablets survive to throw light on Cerialis' successors as garrison commander. The prefect Priscinus may have arrived with the Tungrians in autumn 105. At any rate, he probably served at Vindolanda not much later than Cerialis, since he received letters from Oppius Niger (295) and Caecilius September (298), who had also been correspondents of Cerialis. Only in Niger's letter does a meaningful text survive (quoted in chapter 4, above). It helpfully shows that Priscinus was commanding the First Tungrians and had sent two men to Oppius Niger at the fort of Bremetennacum (Ribchester), bearing a letter for the governor; Niger reports that the great man had already left – perhaps for the *colonia* at Lindum. The beginning of a draft letter from Priscinus to a man called Celsus (1332) might even be a version of the letter in question – on the hypothesis that the governor after Neratius Marcellus was Publilius Celsus – but a likelier identification is Valerius Celsus, prefect of a cavalry regiment.[38]

Another letter to Priscinus (297), surely the same man, was from a brother-officer named Firminus. It opens with a self-justificatory statement: 'I did nothing in a bad spirit. I indeed [?swear that I] did the same in the transaction . . . ' What follows is too fragmentary to give any connected sense, except possibly for the phrase 'a moderate man's sense of decency' – although it could equally mean 'a troublesome man's shame'. This is not much to go on. By way of compensation a fragmentary letter (1491), which must have been written to Priscinus' wife and is surely from a female correspondent, has some nice personal details:

> (as?) my Lady has done, whereby you console me eloquently, just as a mother would do. For my soul . . . this state of mind . . . [during these?] days . . . and I was able to convalesce comfortably. As for you . . . what will you do with your Priscinus?

A possible reading of the address on another letter (1331) may even supply the name of Priscinus' wife, Varia. Not much survives of the text, although there is certainly mention of *primo mane*, 'early in the morning', and a reference to a visit by the recipient to the writer, 'when you came to me'. Another, very fragmentary Period IV letter (324) was certainly written by a woman, whose name ended –inna, and the closing greeting reveals that the recipient was also a woman: '[I pray] that you may be very happy, my Lady, and [continue] to love us'. What survives from the beginning of the letter may be a request 'to write back [whether] you have reached Vin[dolanda]'. No doubt the commanders of the Tungrians entertained as much as Cerialis did. A fragmentary tablet from Period IV (203) looks as if it might be part of a dinner menu: '15 August: a pork cutlet, bread, wine, olive oil . . . '

Very little correspondence from Period V has been found. The end of one letter (353) may reveal the name of a commanding officer's wife: 'greet Pacata in my own words and all your people, with whom, my Lord, I pray that you are in good health.' Another fragmentary letter (352) has preserved the name of the recipient, Marcus Cocceius Velox. It is not certain if he was an officer, but it is certainly noteworthy that he is given a *praenomen* – written out in full and not abbreviated M., as was usual. This is the only case of a Roman citizen at Vindolanda being addressed by all 'three names', the *tria nomina* which had become the hallmark of citizen status. The

*111   A letter to Priscinus' wife
(quid agas cum Pris/cino
tuo?, last two lines on
right-hand side: Inv. 1491)*

praenomen was already losing its significance, except for official purposes. Claudia Severa, it may be recalled, called her husband in one letter 'my Aelius', in another 'Brocchus', but not 'Gaius', which is known to have been his *praenomen*.

Religion

Religion was not, of course, just a matter for the officers, but it is convenient to add some comments on it in this chapter. It probably played a major part in the lives of all the people of Vindolanda, although mention of it does not crop up very often in the writing tablets. Fatalis, perhaps a legionary centurion, in a letter (349) to someone at Vindolanda in Period IV, writes that 'if the gods are propitious . . . I will be . . . on the Nones of . . . ', but this is hardly more than a very conventional expression. An unknown fellow-officer who wrote to Cerialis began his letter (265) by reporting that 'I, brother, have consecrated the day of the Kalends by a sacrifice, just as you wished'. The 'day of the Kalends' referred to New Year's Day, a widespread religious festival in the Roman empire over many centuries. Quite why Cerialis had especially wanted his friend to sacrifice remains obscure. The Saturnalia, which preceded the New Year holiday in late December are mentioned in two letters (301, 1503A). Cerialis and no doubt even more so his wife Lepidina celebrated the Matronalia on 1 March and perhaps the birthday of the goddess Minerva on 21 March (1474A). One or more religious festivals were celebrated by his household in June, including on 24 June one for an unnamed goddess, presumably Fors Fortuna, whose feast-day this was. Cerialis donated a *modius* of wine 'through Privatus', probably his slave – but was himself away: he and Lepidina were staying with their friends Brocchus and Severa at Briga (190). A fragmentary letter from Period III (337) may possibly mention the 'fort festivals', *[sac]ra castresia*, but this is not much to go on. A possible interpretation of an entry in Cerialis' *expensa* might mean that on 9 May (in AD 105?) the regiment celebrated the *rosalia signorum*. This ancient rose-festival was generally held in May. A further Period III tablet, a letter (313), contains an intriguing sentence 'the priest, whom I ask that you send to Verecundus the prefect about the fes[tival?]'. At all events, a temple was built by the Batavians, probably for their god Magusanus.

Magusanus, who was identified with Hercules, seems to have been the chief god of the Batavians. He had had a cult-centre at Empel on the River Maas since pre-Roman times; later a temple was erected there, probably in the Flavian period. This was clearly a war-god: following native practice, items of military equipment were deposited as offerings. An altar found at Ruimel near Nijmegen (*CIL* XIII 8771) was set up by the 'highest magistrate of the state of the Batavians', *summus magistra(tus) civitatis Batavor*. He had a more or less Latinised name, Flaus (probably an abbreviated spelling of Flavus, meaning 'blond'), but he was not a Roman citizen, and his father was called Vihimartis, surely Germanic. The dedication was probably made at latest under Claudius or Nero. Magusanus' cult spread – with his very mobile worshippers – further up the Rhine to Bonn, to northern Britain, where a trooper of the

Tungrians set up an altar to him on the Antonine Wall, to Dacia and to Rome itself (with the Horse Guards).[39] Two stones depicting Hercules found at Vindolanda, an altar and a relief,[40] need not, of course, have any connection with Magusanus or with the temple here. (It seems to have been demolished, and the site used for interment of cremation urns, in the later second century.) Later centuries would produce a great variety of deities at Vindolanda (cf. Epilogue).

Of the equestrian officers or possible officers mentioned in the tablets, some are – literally – only a name. Others, such as Flavius Cerialis and his wife Sulpicia Lepidina, and their friends Aelius Brocchus and Claudia Severa, emerge as real personalities. The prefects of the Batavians and Tungrians were perhaps not wholly typical of the equestrian officers as a whole. Some of their colleagues, such as Haterius Nepos, certainly were. All the same, the language of Cerialis' letters 'suggest[s], albeit indecisively, that he was completely Romanized'.[41] There is thus nothing surprising about the content of a remarkable fragment (1606) found in a Period IV level, which one may classify as *litterae commendaticiae*, 'a letter of recommendation', written by some patron presumably on behalf of one of the Vindolanda commanders, probably a prefect of Tungrians. As often happens in such cases, the unknown who was recommended was evidently given a copy of the glowing reference: *[ ] viri boni accedit etiam liberalium studiorum amor e[iu]s profectus morum denique te[m]peramentum et cla[ritas generis?]*, '[qualities] of a good man; added to this is his decided love of liberal studies, finally his balanced character and the [distinction of his family?]'. The language here closely resembles specimens of such letters in the correspondence of the Younger Pliny[42] – indeed, it is not stretching the imagination too far to say that Pliny could have written this letter. Most of these letters are indeed only fragments. We may end with another (1584), perhaps from Period IV: 'I wish all the time . . . I, certainly, at the time of writing this am in good health. It is the third day, brother, that . . . '

112 A glowing reference (Inv. 1606)

8 Epilogue

What happened next? A good deal is known about the Ninth Batavians and the First Tungrians after they left Vindolanda. The Batavians went first to Trajan's war in Dacia. They did not stay in that area long. Soon they were based in Raetia, where they would remain.[1] Eventually, the *Notitia Dignitatum* shows, they were stationed on the upper Danube. Their station took its name from them: *Batava Castra* (Passau). As for the prefects who served at Vindolanda, Flavius Genialis, it was suggested (chapter 7), may have settled in Rome. But Cerialis and Lepidina disappear from view. It is not even known if Cerialis took the regiment to the Dacian war. He might easily have handed over command to a new prefect, for example when they reached the Rhine island on their long journey, to retire into civilian life or to be given a new command. His friend Brocchus has left a trace: he dedicated an altar, appropriately to Diana, the huntress, at Arrabona in Pannonia. There he was prefect of cavalry, perhaps of a new elite double-strength regiment just raised by Trajan, the *ala Ulpia contariorum milliaria*, known to have been stationed at Arrabona. Brocchus may have owed his appointment to Neratius Priscus, Marcellus' brother, governor of Pannonia during the Second Dacian war.[2]

The Tungrians were probably still at Vindolanda until the 140s: a man discharged in 146 after 25 years service in the regiment left his bronze diploma in the fort. By the Severan period, at the latest, they were at Housesteads, and remained there until the end. But they had probably changed station more than once between these postings.[3] Much had changed in the meantime. Hadrian's Wall had been built, which must have affected Vindolanda. A visit by Hadrian in 122 seems probable, as argued earlier. And an inscription (*RIB* 1701) has been found here of the man left to direct the building of Hadrian's Wall, Platorius Nepos. Nepos, it was suggested, might even have stayed at Vindolanda for some time. With thousands of legionaries in the neighbourhood, most quartered in temporary camps, some a short way west along the Stanegate, things must have been lively, not least for civilian traders in the *vicus*.

The Wall was soon evacuated in favour of a renewed occupation of southern Scotland, and the new Antonine Wall was built, occupied for two decades, then given up again.[4] Vindolanda continued to be held throughout. It was rebuilt in stone, at a reduced size, more or less on the site of the Tungrians' first fort, at the eastern edge of the plateau, some time between 130 and 160.[5] The Tungrians presumably left before the stone fort was built: it was too small for a milliary cohort, if there at full strength. Various inscriptions found at or near Vindolanda may hint at the new garrison. Two altars, one dedicated to the local British god Cocidius by Decimus

113   Martius to Victor his dearest brother (Inv. 1215)

Caerellius Victor, prefect of the Second Cohort of Nervians (*RIB* 1683), the other to Mars Victor by Caninius, prefect of the Third Cohort of Nervians (*RIB* 1691), suggest that at some time these units were based here. There is no indication of date in either case.

The later history of Vindolanda has not as yet been brought to life by any writing tablets – with one exception. One found in a Period VIA level (1215), datable *c*.180–200, is a letter from Martius to Victor. It might, of course, have been shifted from an earlier level during Roman building operations, as is the case with some other tablets. But the style of handwriting supports the dating in the late second century, several generations after the other tablets. The address has the locative place-name *Coris*, suggesting (on the interpretation adopted here) that it was written at Coria (Corbridge). Victor's rank is given by an expression ending *eq(uitum)*, 'of cavalry', or *eq(uitis)*, 'cavalryman' – what precedes this, on the previous line, is missing. It might be possible to restore *pr(aefecto)*. In that case, Victor might have been commanding a cavalry regiment stationed at Vindolanda in the Antonine or early Severan Period. On the other hand, Martius appears to assume that Victor was at Bremenium, north of the Wall, and that he would soon be at Cataractonium, on the road from Coria to Eburacum.

114   The address on Martius' letter (Inv. 1215)

At all events, the rather fragmentary text is worth citing:

> Martius to Victor his dearest brother greeting. Know that it is well with me,
> which I wish in turn for you. I am making you agent, brother, . . . the
> relatives of my (?) father . . . carefully and that they may not divide . . . you
> . . . what you are in need of, that the matter is dealt with. I ask you to write
> to me through an *optio*. If you do not have an *optio* at Bremenium, give (it)
> at Cataractonium to Durm[. . .] the veteran, or to .esarius. In . . . we had
> been. Greet Proculus and his(?) family and . . . onitis, your(?) daughter, and
> Valentinus the *vexillarius* and . . . anus.
> [on the back]: At Coria(?). To Victor [prefect?] of cavalry, from Ma[rtius].

In the early third century something very curious happened at Vindolanda. The
entire fort was levelled and dozens of circular, stone huts were erected, in neat rows.
They were clearly not to house Roman troops. It had something to do with Severus'
expedition. He was in Britain from 208-11 with a vast expeditionary force, intending
to reconquer all north Britain – a return to the policy of Agricola (or Domitian).
Native Britons were surely quartered at Vindolanda: hostages from Caledonia,

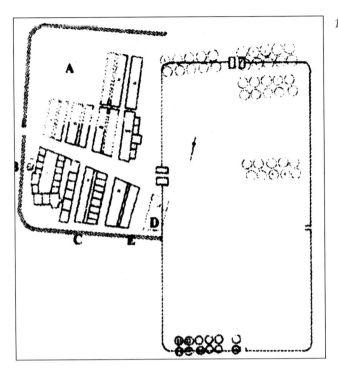

115 *Vindolanda in the early third century: round huts for refugees or hostages?*

116 *How the round huts might have looked*

perhaps, or pro-Roman refugees, for example Votadini, rescued from anti-Roman neighbours? At the same time a replacement fort to accommodate Roman troops was erected, with its long axis east and west. What was originally thought to be a *mansio* for travellers can now be understood as the *praetorium* of this new fort; the 'married quarters', as they were first interpreted, were standard barracks.

This strange arrangement was soon done away with. The round huts were levelled to the foundations and a standard stone fort was built again.[6] The garrison was now the Fourth Cohort of Gauls, part-mounted, paper strength 600 men. They were to remain until the end of Roman rule. Since Trajan's day, their first attestation in Britain, they had changed station again and again: first in Yorkshire, to the Wall in Hadrian's reign, to the Antonine Wall, then to Bremenium in the later second century.[7] They were at Vindolanda at latest in 213: like numerous other regiments in the province that year, they asserted their loyalty to Caracalla. A dedication-slab in the headquarters building was set up out of the cohort's 'joint duty and devotion', *pr[o pietate a]c devotione communi* (*RIB* 1704). Probably in the next year, Britain was divided into two provinces. Everything up to the frontier zone, from a line south of Lincoln and north of Chester, was separated off, as Lower Britain, with the legate of the Sixth legion at Eburacum becoming the governor.[8] This may not have made much difference to Vindolanda. Provincial headquarters were nearer, not necessarily a welcome change.

Ten years or so later, 'devoted to the divine spirit' of the young Emperor Severus Alexander, the Fourth Gauls rebuilt the south gate, with its towers (*RIB* 1706). Several third-century prefects dedicated altars in the *praetorium*. Pituanius Secundus set up his to the *Genius praetori* alone, the 'spirit' of this building (*RIB* 1685), Quintus Petronius Urbicus, 'from Italy, his home-town Brixia' (Brescia) (1686), to 'Jupiter Best and Greatest and the other immortal gods' as well. A third prefect, perhaps called Caecilius Celer, also offered his altar (1687) to Jupiter and the Genius (omitting *praetori*), and added 'the guardian gods'.

 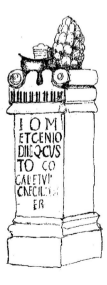

117 The altars from the praetorium, *as drawn by John Hodgson*

118   *Gaius Julius Raeticus worships the fortune of the Roman People*
      (replica: the centurial sign has not been shown)

119   An altar to the Veteres from Vindolanda   *120   The vicani Vindolandesses erect an altar to Vulcan*

Religion, relatively sparsely recorded in the writing tablets, is much more to the fore in the later period. Altars reveal a string of deities and in some cases their worshippers. Jupiter Best and Greatest was honoured on three, probably all set up by prefects, but only one name has survived, Pudens (*RIB* 1688, cf. 1689-90). A centurion of VI Victrix, Gaius Julius Raeticus, perhaps acting commander of the Fourth Gauls, erected a fine altar to the Fortune of the Roman People (1684). Nameless worshippers honoured the Mothers, Mercury and Neptune (1692-4). Aurelius Modestus, '*beneficiarius* of the Upper province's Consular', seconded to the north, was a keen hunter, it may be assumed: he worshipped the god of the wild, Silvanus (1696).

A strange deity, unknown elsewhere in the Roman Empire, is recorded on over 50 little altars from the frontier region, five at Vindolanda. Virtually all were dedicated by humble folk. There are more than a dozen variant spellings of the deity. A plural form, *Veteribus* or *dibus veteribus*, seems to mean 'the Old Gods'; *deo Veteri*, 'the Old God', is also found. Other variants betray non-Latin origin, including *Hveteribus, Hvitiribus* in the plural, *Vetiri, Vetri, Vitiri, Hveteri, Hvitri, Vheteri* in the singular. These spellings, especially with *Hv-* or *Vh-*, show that the name could not readily be expressed in the Latin alphabet. This may be an ancient local spirit, ill-defined as to number (and even sex: two examples honour the *Vitires* as female), or perhaps originally a Germanic import – brought by the Batavians or Tungrians? Odin or Woden had the epithet *vithrir*, god of 'weather', no bad presiding spirit for the northern borderlands. Otherwise, the name might be connected with Old Nordic *hvitr*, 'white' or 'shining', or *hvethr-ung*, 'son of a giantess', applied to Loki, the equivalent of Vulcan.[9] This protector of smiths and craftsmen was worshipped at Vindolanda. The inhabitants of the *vicus* made a corporate dedication to him for the

121 Constantine in AD 309/10 (coin found at Vindolanda)

'divine family' of the imperial house and 'for the spirits of the emperors', *Pro domu divina et numinibus Augustorum Volcano sacrum vicani Vindolandesses* (*RIB* 1700).

The 'Old God(s)' suggests conservatism or reaction in the face of new religions. Mithras, Isis and other 'oriental' cults have not yet surfaced at Vindolanda. The eastern cult that was to outdo all others started its triumphal progress not so far away, at Eburacum in 306, with Constantine's elevation, so he later proclaimed (Eusebius, *Vita Const.* 2.28). The spread was mainly in the other direction: it probably took a long time for the faith to travel the 125 Roman miles to the Wall. But there is now evidence for Christianity at least in the latest phase of the *praetorium*, and, with Brigomaglos, in sub-Roman times (see chapter 1).

Notes

1 Introduction

1   Jackson 1982 on Brigomaglos, with a better text and dismissing the identification once claimed with St Brioc (Brieuc); the name means 'high chief' or 'mighty prince'; cf. Birley, R. *et al.* 1999: 22f., with further bibliography. The tombstone was found in 1889; not *in situ*, but in a pile of loose stones outside Chesterholm house. Cf. Bidwell 1985: 76, also discussing the pennanular brooch, with double snake-heads, found at the south gate in 1969; Birley, R. 1970: 136 and fig. 1 no. 2. Later identified (Bidwell 1985: 38, with further references) as 'an early Anglo-Saxon type with parallels of sixth- or seventh-century date'. Chapel: Birley, R. *et al.* 1999: 20ff. *Chi-rho* stone: Birley, A. & Blake 2000: 9f. and figs. 8-9.

2   Ninth-century strap-end (found in 1980): Birley, R. *et al.* 1998: 5f. and fig. 4; cf. *ibid.* for a concise account of post-Roman activity in the area; and 19ff. on Hedley's *praetorium* excavation. There is also a concise summary on research at Vindolanda in *VRR* IV.1: 4ff. Cf. also Bidwell 1985: 76 (who registers the lost penny). On Hedley and early excavations see esp. Birley, R. 1995 (the quotation is from p.14 – Hedley had Great Chesters, Housesteads and the outpost fort Risingham on Dere Street in mind for his 'blitz-excavation', rather than the fort he owned himself); Chesterholm, Birley, R. 2000.

3   For refs to the first publication see *RIB*. A small excavation near the findspot, by Thomas Hepple, was not productive: still commemorated there by a laconic report, on stone: the date and 'Nothing found'.

4   Birley, E. 1961: 146f., 185ff., with bibliography of his excavation reports. Cf. also Birley, R. 1977: 103; Bidwell 1985: 34ff.

5   Reports in Birley, R.: 1962; 1970; 1973.

6   Birley, R. 1977: 29ff.; 170ff.; Birley, R. 1995: 63ff.

7   The quotation is from his own account, Birley, R. 1977: 132. Cf. *ibid*. 103ff., 132-57 for further details on the 1973-5 seasons; most of the writing tablets were still unpublished when he wrote (and remained so until 1983).

8   It was inventoried as no. 15 in the first series. Cf. the introduction to *TV* I 38: it 'was the first [tablet] to be recognised as such . . . It was unavoidably damaged in an early attempt at conservation.' First publication: Bowman, Thomas & Wright 1974: 474ff.

9   Full details in Birley, R. 1977: esp. 104ff.; id. 1994: 13 ('On some mornings it was necessary to pump for three to four hours before excavation could be resumed, removing 6,000 gallons each hour.') My account here is no more than a selective sketch.

10 Two examples may be given. It was claimed that a large area had been cleared by machine in 1973, without archaeological examination. In fact, this was carried out by the County Council, outside the Trust's land (and outside the area with ancient remains), to create a car park. Also in 1973, sixth-formers under my direction were cleaning out, in preparation for photography, the ditch of the late stone fort, where it had gone through earlier levels and I was straightening the section at the north end of the trench, when the Principal Inspector of Ancient

Monuments for England and Wales arrived. He peered down, demanded to know where the Director was, and left abruptly after a few minutes, without asking any other questions. He was later to claim on the basis of this visit that the writing tablets were being excavated by schoolchildren, with spades, in waterlogged trenches which were being emptied by buckets.

11 For the history of Carvoran: Birley, R. 1998.

12 A 'kleine Sensation': B. Galsterer-Kröll at the start of her review in the *Bonner Jahrbücher* 1988: 655; 'exemplary', her concluding sentence, *ibid.*: 658.

13 A full listing in *VRR* II: Appendix 2, 109ff. (The concordance in *TV* II: pp. 367ff. omits 'non-tablets', blank and stylus tablets.)

14 Cf. Birley, A.R. 1991A: 16, reporting (in September 1989) on plans for publication; or id. 1991B: 87 n.3.

15 Birley, R. & Birley, A. 1994: the texts are Inv. 1022, 1091A, 1108, 1187.

16 Bowman & Thomas 1996 (the quotation is from p.299). That paper also includes (326ff.) a slight, but important revised reading of Inv. 1022, line 7: not *spicá* but *si itá*. Interpretation of the content of this letter (by a man called Major) remains open to debate (cf. chapter 5, below).

17 Cf. Birley, R. 1999A for such a publication (the first edition appeared in 1990).

18 *TV* II: p. 19.

19 Cf. Birley, A.R. 1991: 16-20 (a summary, from September 1989, of the original draft of *VRR* II 18-72; it was revised a little in 1991-2 to take account of new finds). *VRR* II was reviewed briefly (and somewhat patronisingly), jointly with *TV* II, the latter at great length and, as it deserved, very favourably, by Tomlin 1996 (making some valuable suggestions for improvements).

20 Birley, A.R. 1998; more briefly in Birley R. *et al.* 1998: 54ff.

21 Birley, R. *et al.* 1998: 7; 1999: 27f.

22 Birley, A. & Blake 2000; Birley, A. 2001; Blake 2001.

23 Bowman & Thomas 1983: 44f.; Birley, R. 1999A: 10ff. (In neither is the thickness mentioned.)

24 The Latin word is *stilus*, hence the spelling 'stylus' is strictly speaking incorrect. But as with 'style', also derived from *stilus*, 'stylus' seems to have established itself as the English name. (Bowman & Thomas 1983, *TV* I, write 'stylus', 1994, *TV* II, 'stilus'.)

25 Birley, R. 1999A: 8.

26 Tomlin 1998; for the tiny handful of previously known leaf tablets cf. Bowman & Thomas 1983: 34ff.

27 Cf. Locher & Rottländer 1985, discussing Pliny, *Nat.Hist.* 16.68, which they convincingly emend in the light of 16. 226 and 229. Cf. Bowman & Thomas 1983: 30; and 41ff. on passages in other Greek and Latin authors that probably refer to leaf tablets; also id. 1994: 40ff.

28 Birley, R. 1999A: 17ff.

29 This tablet is not illustrated in *TV* II.

30 Cf. e.g. Birley, A.R. 1993: 61, suggesting that the letter as we have it was only a draft; approved by Speidel, M.A. 1996: 39 n. 45. As he points out, we cannot properly call this an 'address', since nothing else was written along with it, not even the name of the recipient (Candidus).

31 The quotations are from Bowman & Thomas 1994: 43 and Birley, A.R. 2001A: n. 16.

32 Adams 1995: 109, citing Michigan Papyrus VIII 467.25, a letter from Claudius Terentianus to Claudius Tiberianus.

33 For arguments in favour of the place-name being the place of delivery, see Bowman & Thomas 1994: 42ff.; Adams 1995: 108ff.; Tomlin 1996: 460. For the

other view, that the place-name referred to the place of writing, see Speidel, M.A. 1996: 38f.; Birley, A.R. 1999: 43f.; 2001A: 248ff.

34 This is not the place to give a complete list. But cf. also e.g. Cicero to his wife and daughter, ending *Menturnis, Formiis,* or *de Venusino* (*Ad fam.* 14.14, 18, 20).

35 *CIL* XIII 3162; Birley, A.R. 1981: 188ff.

36 *ILS* 5918a.

37 For the first example (Domitian), *CIL* IX 5420. For the others, mostly in Greek, some in Latin as well, see Oliver 1989: nos. 28, 55, 56, 58B, 68, 74, 74bis, 79-82, 128, 136, 142-153, 177, 182, 204, 215, 250A, 268, 285.

2 Batavians and Tungrians

1 See Roymans 1996.

2 Neumann 1976: 91. For a different interpretation of the name (to mean '[people of the] good water-meadow') cf. Willems 1986: 210, with references. This would imply that the immigrants only acquired the name on arrival in the Rhine island.

3 See Roymans 2001 for a detailed examination of these coins.

4 Speidel 1994: 13ff.

5 Alföldy 1968: 45ff.; Strobel 1987.

6 Holder 1980: 46ff.; 1982: 51ff.

7 Willems 1986: 234ff.

8 Hassall 1970: esp. 134f.

9 Speidel, M.P. 1994: 29f.

10 Birley, A.R. 1981: 225ff.

11 Strobel 1987: 284f.

12 For this view, cf. Holder 1982: 64f.; Strobel 1987: 273 n. 19; Birley, A.R. 1990A: 335; 1993: 45; Saddington 1991: 414; Devijver 1976-1993 F43 bis (vol. V, p. 2104); Bowman 1994: 27; Bowman & Thomas 1994: 25; Adams 1995: 129; Birley, A.R. 2001a: 250f.; 2001b:16.

13 Grünewald (forthcoming).

14 Holder 1982: 111, 122f.

15 Holder 1980: 5ff. is the best discussion of unit strength and organisation. Cf. also Holder 1982: 20ff., 28ff.

16 Strobel 1987: 287ff. and cf. p.61 below.

17 On the salaries of equestrian officers: Devijver 1989: 408f. On soldiers' pay: Speidel, M.A. 1992: 87ff.

18 See esp. Breeze 1974: 245ff.

19 Cf. for most of these Index IV to TV II, pp. 394f. For Masclus: Bowman & Thomas 1996: 323ff.; seplasiarius: Inv. 1495; signifer: Inv. 836 (stylus), cf. *VRR* II 25.

3 Vindolanda

1 Cf. Birley, E. 1963 for the quarries being worked early in Hadrian's reign.

2 Rivet & Smith 1979: 500, 502.

3 Ross 1967: 19ff.

4 Rivet & Smith 1979: 317ff., 329, 470ff. The goddess' name, in the dative, is taken to be Sattadae in *RIB*, with tt marked as uncertain; for Saitadae cf. Ross 1967: 228, 231 and Birley, E. 1986: 71, both citing K.H. Jackson. (The lettering, rather worn, actually looks more like Saiiadae.)

5 Birley, A.R. 2001C: 17ff.
6 For these peoples Rivet & Smith 1979: 249f., 278ff., 301f., 322, 455, 508f.; cf. also Birley, A.R. 2001C.
7 On Milking Gap, Clarke 1958: 62f.
8 Bidwell 1999: 11ff. summarises present thinking and evidence for what happened in AD 105. See also p.69, 135 below.
9 Keppie 2000A: 90ff.
10 Jones, G.D.B 1991, although open to criticism in detail, remains valuable; cf. id. 1989.
11 Speidel, M.P. 1998.
12 References for these places are provided in later chapters.
13 Seaward 1993: 94.
14 Cf. Bidwell 1985: 4, drawing attention to two large blocks of sandstone, the larger weighing over 2.5 tonnes, with wedge-holes on its upper surface, in the south part of Chesterholm gardens; indeed, sitting in the Chineley Burn. They might have come from the Barcombe quarry, as he observes. But just as likely is that they came from the cliff a few feet away from where it lies, on the east side of the Chineley Burn – and they could have been first quarried by Anthony Hedley's builders in the 1820s. Bidwell is agnostic as to the source of the softer, yellow or buff sandstone. Robin Birley points out to me that this stone – which was extensively used in pre-Hadrianic period – probably came from the Brackies Burn, where stone was certainly won, only about 200m north-west of the fort.
15 Seaward 1993: 95. His experiments indicated that bracken spread straight onto a floor and trampled on for some weeks created a very unpleasant smell. He suggests that, to avoid this, the Romans air-dried the bracken before spreading it.
16 Pearce forthcoming is the fullest recent discussion of the food eaten at Vindolanda. Cf. the pioneering studies by Hodgson 1976 and 1977; and Seaward 1993: 103ff. ; and (summarising Hodgson) 108ff.

4 Tungrians, Batavians and Tungrians again

1 On Bolanus and Petillius: Birley, A.R. 1981: 62ff. Hassall 2000: 51ff. is now the best guide to the stations of the legions at this time; cf. also Keppie 2000B.
2 On Petillius' campaigns Caruana 1997 and Shotter 2000 come to similar conclusions by different routes.
3 On the chronology of Agricola's governorship: Birley, A.R. 1981: 77ff., confirmed, with refinements in detail, by Raepsaet-Charlier 1991: esp. 1842, 1857.
4 Tomlin 1998: 74f.; 1992: 146ff.
5 Jones, B.W. 1992: 18ff., 128ff. (with full bibliography).
6 Cf. Breeze & Dobson 2000: 10ff.; Hassall 2000: 54ff., 62ff. Cohh. I & II Batavorum: Strobel 1987: 275ff.
7 Tomlin 1998: 74f., no. 44.
8 The existence of Roman structures north of the present line of the Stanegate seems guaranteed by traces on aerial photographs taken by the late Barri Jones, confirmed by the geophysical survey conducted in 2000. Further, an early east-west ditch, which could be the southern ditch of this postulated first fort at Vindolanda, was found to underlie the temple excavated in 2001.
9 In spite of emphatic statements to the contrary, there is no strong reason to doubt that *TV* II 154 belongs to Period I. It is naturally possible that it was displaced into the Period I ditch from Period II, or, as Birley, R. 1994 (in

VRR I): 24 n. 9, notes, 'Tablets 837, 839, 840 and 841 [=*TV* II 161, 302, 496, 154] may have come from a Period II pit.' This is mentioned as a possibility (no more) in a footnote in *VRR* II: 23 n.2; in the discussion, *ibid.* 23ff., the tablets' origin in period I is taken to be more probable. Bowman & Thomas 1994: 91 write that '[i]t now appears much more likely that the material in this [Period I] ditch was produced by the occupants of Period 2 [citing *VRR* II: 23 n.2], which would place the presence of Julius Verecundus and the Tungrians at Vindolanda in the years c.92-7.' (A similar view is repeated briefly in Bowman 1994: 22.)

10 Excavation in 2001 revealed three outer ditches, at a distance which allows one to postulate a further two between them and the innermost western ditch; and from excavation on the north side of the stone fort it was clear that the north ditches of the Period I-IV forts must lie south of the stone fort wall. A deep fill of mainly whinstone boulders, similar to that found in the Period I west ditch, was found under the stone fort praetorium: Birley, R. *et al.* 1998: 7. It is not certain to which of the pre-Hadrianic forts this feature belonged. Period I south ditch: Blake 2001: 21f.

11 Birley, R. 1994: 15ff.

12 Blake 2001: 21f. and figs. 31-2.

13 Birley, E. 1993: 6f. This interpretation is rejected by Tomlin, 1996: 461, but I am not convinced by his arguments. Training did not have to take place 'at a rearward base', as he claims. See also next note.

14 The alternative explanation by Tomlin, 1996: 461 of why the commanders of the two Tungrian cohorts stationed in Britain continued to be called prefect, not tribune, even when the units were double-strength, is less convincing than that of Strobel, 1987: 287ff., followed here.

15 I see no reason to suppose that the Ninth Batavians were stationed at Vindolanda together with the First Tungrians, as is sometimes suggested. This depends on the belief that the Tungrians' strength report, although found in the period I ditch, really belongs to period II; cf. n.9 above.

16 Strobel 1987: 280ff.

17 Strobel 1987: 287f. cites *Sever[us, pra]efect(us) coh. III Batavorum (=milliariae) eq(uitatae)*, *AE* 1969/70. 526, Vetus Salina, Pannonia and a dedication by *coh. IX Ba[t.] eq. (=milliaria) expl(oratorum)* under M. Victorius Provincialis *praef(ectus)*. *CIL* III.11818=ILS 9152, Weissenburg (Bavaria), in the province of Raetia. Cf. Devijver 1976-93: S 100, V 112. Both were probably Batavians – this is clear for the wife of the prefect of the Third, [R]omana, whose home is given as [Ulpia Nov]iomagi, Nijmegen. Cf. also Devijver 1979-95: S 101.

18 See below

19 Birley, R. 1994: 36ff.

20 Birley, R. 1994: 39ff.; on the bracken carpeting see also Seaward 1993: 93ff.

21 Birley, R. 1994: 51ff.

22 Birley, R. 1993: 92, no. 2; Driel-Murray 1993: 64, no. 7.

23 CIL XVI 48; Birley, A.R. 1981: 87ff.

24 Information from Justin Blake, who carried out the excavation.

25 My provisional reading of the Vindolanda altar is: DEO/ MA. /V..NO. On Magusanus, cf. further below, chapter 7.

26 Jones, B.W. 1993: 193ff.

27 Syme 1958: 1ff. remains the best account of Nerva's short reign.

28 Speidel, M.P. 1994: 37ff.

29 On the Neratii brothers: *PIR2* N 50, 60. Priscus and Cerialis: Birley, A.R. 1991: 97ff.

30 Birley, R. 1994: 53ff.

31 Birley, Andrew 2001: 12ff., 15ff., 47ff.; animal-prints: Higgs 2001.
32 For this and what follows, Birley, R. 1994: 54ff.
33 Birley, R. 1994: 87f.
34 For limited traces of the early forts found in 1999 and 2000, under the stone fort, see Birley, A. & Blake 2000: 6ff.; Blake 2001: 12ff., 20f.
35 Birley, R. 1994: 58ff. and figs. 22-3.
36 Birley, R. 1994: 62ff.
37 Birley, R. 1994: 75ff.
38 Birley, R. 1994: 89f.
39 *Inscriptiones Daciae Romanae* II 562, 572. For AD 105, cf. further chapter 7 below.
40 Demolition, double barrack-block, south gate: Birley, R. 1994: 90ff., 108 and figs. 28-30; information on the possible Period IV *praetorium* or Period V structure comes from the excavations of 2001; to be continued in 2002.
41 Birley, R. 1994: 92ff. His chronology is slightly modified here.
42 *HA, Hadr.* 5.2: 'the Britons could not be kept under Roman control'.
43 Birley, A.R. 1998.
44 Birley, A.R. 2001C.
45 ILS 2726.
46 Fronto, *De bello Parthico* 2, 220f. van den Hout; discussed in Birley, A.R. 1998.
47 See now Eck 1999.
48 Birley, A.R. 1998; Keppie 2000A: 83ff., 2000B: 29 (sceptical about the Ninth legion ending up in the east).
49 HA, Hadr. 11.1. Cf. Breeze & Dobson 2000: 25ff.
50 Birley, A.R. 1981: 100ff.; 221f.; 273f.
51 Birley, A.R. 1997B: 102f. Cf. e.g. *HA, Hadr.* 9.8, 17.6-8, 20.1 ('in conversation even with the humblest he behaved very much as an ordinary citizen') or Cassius Dio 69.6.3.
52 Birley, A.R. 1997B: 135. Cf. further chapter 6, below.
53 Birley, R. 1994: 113ff. and fig. 31, 125f. and fig. 32.
54 *VRR* II: 91 no. 1 and fig. 9.3.
55 Fully discussed by Roxan 1985; summarised in her notes to RIB II 2401.9.
56 Cf. the Epilogue (ch. 8).

5 Military routine

1 Birley, A.R. 1981: 82ff.; Speidel, M.A. 1995.
2 Jones, B.W. 1992: 133ff., 141f., 144ff., 182. II Adiutrix: Keppie 2000B: 28; Hassall 2000: 62f. (suggesting that II Adiutrix, not XX, had actually been the legion at Inchtuthil).
3 *CIL* XVI 54, cf. Birley, E. 1953: 22; Speidel, M.P. 1987: 127; Jones, B.W. 1993: 134.
4 Kajanto 1965: 267 found just over 50 men called Ferox. Cf. Lörincz 1999: 139.
5 For the reading *stipendiatum*: Tomlin 1996: 461.
6 *RIB* II 2446 publishes the oculists' stamps found in Britain, with valuable introduction. Nos. 2c, 4b, 11b(?), 19a, 22a, 23d, 27b offered remedies for *lippitudo*.
7 Adams 1995: 102f., correcting *TV* II 127-153, where the editors still take *qui debunt* as *q(ui) videbunt*. See below for the reason, Masclus' spelling of *habunt*.
8 Preliminary publication by Bowman & Thomas 1996: 323ff.
9 Cf. Birley, A.R. 2001B: 252f.
10 This tablet was not published in *TV* II.
11 The place-name Ulucium is not previously recorded, but the obviously misspelt 'Vividin' in the *Ravenna Cosmography* (Rivet & Smith 1979: 213,

507) could easily have been corrupted from this: VLVCIVM misread as VIVIDIN. As 'Vividin' is listed three entries after one for the River Tyne and two entries before for those for the River Aln and Coquet, a location in Northumberland is plausible. For a possible large Trajanic fort at Newbrough: Jones, G.D.B. 1991: 100ff.

12 Tacitus, *Annals* 1.35.1; *Hist.* 1.46; and see Speidel, M.P. 1992: 330ff.

13 Tomlin 1998: 55ff., no. 16, 74f., no. 44.

14 1361 allows the reading of Cluvius' second name to be corrected in *TV* II 281, where *Fabro*, ablative, is read; *Floro* is correct.

15 The tablet was first published by Birley, R. & Birley, A. 1994: 435ff. The reading here quoted is a more recent attempt of my own.

16 I previously suggested that the two might have been half-brothers, from Salonae in Dalmatia: Birley, A.R. 1990: 6f. This possibility depends among other things on Adiutor's *nomen* being 'Vettius'. In *TV* II the editors read it as 'Vittius', but I still prefer 'Vettius'.

17 Funari 1991.

18 Cf. Driel-Murray 1993: 54ff.

19 *CIL* III 11818=*ILS* 9152, Weissenburg (Bavaria), a dedication by their prefect M. Victorius Provincialis (cf. Devijver 1976-93: V 112).

20 See *VRR* IV.1.

21 Birley, A.R. 1979: 101ff.

22 The above summarises (with slight modifications) Birley, A.R. 2001C.

23 *AE* 1979. 388. Cf. Holder 1982: 107; Birley, A.R. 1997B: 134. There is room for dispute about the regiment's identity and when it won its title.

6 The soldiers

1 The names are discussed in detail in Birley, A.R. 2001A. It need hardly be added that the reading of some of them will need to be revised. To the bibliography in that article (259f.) add Lörincz & Redö 1994, Lörincz 1999, 2000.

2 *VRR* II: 55; Speidel, M.P. 1994: 155; Birley, A.R. 2001A: 257f.

3 I am grateful to Jim Adams for discussing *gratulatus sum* (to mean just 'I am glad that', rather than 'I have congratulated'). The last sentence is my own reading, differing from that in *TV* II, of lines 11-14: *scis certe hoc me rite impetrare cum sim nonanus etiam adep[tus] translationem.* (Cf. also for yet another version Tomlin 1996: 462f.) It is not easy to detect the symbol for centurion read by the editors after Super's name in the address.

4 I prefer this reading of the name to 'Ircucisso' in *TV* II. 'Proucisso' is a possible alternative.

5 Driel-Murray 1993: 9ff., 65.

6 *RIB* 1420, supposed to have been found at Housesteads.

7 On this point see especially Adams 1995: 87, 94, 95, 101, 108.

8 For what follows cf. Birley, A.R. 1991: 93f.; and *VRR* II: 59ff.

9 *RIB* 2082, where the second name should be read as Seranus rather than Sebanus.

10 Ti. Claudius Fatalis' funerary inscription is *AE* 1939, 157. The editors of *TV* II 349 state that the traces of the incompletely preserved *gentilicium* of the Fatalis who wrote this letter 'do not favour' *[Clau]dio*. They do not publish the photograph, inspection of which suggests that *-dio* is a perfectly possible reading.

11 Glico: *RIB* 2164, Croy Hill. Firmus: *RIB* 2174-7; and see Birley, E. 1953: 83-103.

12 For this interpretation, differing from that in *TV* II, cf. Birley, A.R. 1997A: 276f.; 1997B: 135.

13 It was originally published by Birley, R. & A. 1994: 440ff. Bowman & Thomas 1996: 326ff. corrected a few readings, in particular in line 7, where their *si ita* is clearly correct (rather than *spica*); and in line 14 *bracem* may be correct (rather than *Britem*). But their reading of the recipient's name as *Coccelio* rather than *Cocceiio* must be rejected, as also their interpretation of *fussa* as a 'spindle' – other considerations aside, such objects could easily have been made at Vindolanda, and could hardly have been the subject of a letter in these terms. I owe the interpretation of *fussa* as the past participle of *fundo*, with *brace* understood, to Jim Adams. In Birley, R. & A. 1994: 440ff. an almost similar view was taken, but with the mistaken reading *spica* – and it was incorrectly translated 'spilled' rather than 'poured', as Jim Adams also points out. I hope that he will before long publish an improved interpretation of this letter. It need hardly be added that Bowman & Thomas take a different view on the meaning of the place-name in the address, in this as in other cases.

7 The officers and their families

1 Most of the individuals in this chapter are fully discussed in Birley, A.R. 2001B. Some corrections to readings there are required.
2 For this explanation of *souxtum*, see Adams 1996.
3 I previously read Gentilis' name, in the dative, as *Cenosi* (Birley, A.R. 2001B: 17); for *Gentili*, Birley, A.R. 2001C: 16 – but there, alas, I not only mistakenly still assert that 1449 joins 1434, but again misread 1449, as *amico a Vegeto Genialis*. David Thomas' superior skills have corrected this (as Jim Adams kindly tells me), reading *Vegetus Geniali domino* (this word inserted on line above) *su[o]*; I am not sure if he will accept *Gentili* in 1434, but that I would retain. As for the text on the other side of 1434, of which some four or five lines are faintly visible, I am unable to read more than one or two individual letters and these without much confidence.
4 *CIL* VI 35284.
5 *PIR2* F 277.
6 One of these belonged to the upper class of the Greek city of Perinthus and the other was assumed, when his existence was first made known, to come from the east as well, since origin in the west seemed unlikely, cf. Birley, A.R. 2001B: 27f.
7 Birley, A.R. 1991: 97f.
8 Pliny, *Letters* 3.8.
9 Cf. Birley, A.R. 1991: 99f.
10 Adams 1995: 129 comments that this letter 'presents the most formal and literary Latinity' in all the Vindolanda tablets, with 'consistently correct orthography . . . two types of old-fashioned spelling' and 'an accumulation of formal literary phrases, word order and syntax of a type which cannot simply be explained as manifesting hackneyed epistolary clichés'.
11 My translation differs slightly here and there from that of the editors in *TV* II.
12 In Birley, A.R. 1991: 95 n. 39 it is suggested that Crispinus was a tribune of senatorial status or a legionary legate in Britain. Tomlin 1996: 462 agrees that Crispinus was of senatorial rank, but argues that he was not in Britain, but elsewhere, perhaps at Rome, because Cerialis calls Marcellus 'my Consular', not '*our* Consular'. This is hardly a compelling argument and, if Crispinus were not in Britain, how was he to greet Marcellus, evidently still governor and thus in the province?
13 This interpretation differs in several respects from that of the editors. Bowman & Thomas 1996: 308 state that 'examination of the physical characteristics of the leaves has enabled us to reconstruct the sequence of the leaves and the format of the text'.

However, it seems perfectly possible that the leaves, originally six, joined and folded in concertina format, were separated into individual sheets before use by the writer. The editors' own order produces a puzzling chronology: both lines 1-43/4, which they call 'Section 1 (incoming)', and 46-the end, their 'Section 2 (outgoing)', cover the years 102-4. I prefer to take their line 65 as marking a consular date, 1 January AD 102, reading *k(alendis) Ianuaris Ser[viano II cos.]*, rather than *per[. . .]* (the former is a perfectly possible reading, as the editors concede) and to make the sheet in which this entry occurs, their 'E back', the first, while retaining the order of the remainder. This produces a chronology going from 10 June 101 to 16 July 105. A further sheet, written on both sides, may be missing for the period mid-June (end of 'sheet D') AD 104 to mid-March (beginning of 'sheet D back') 105. On a further aspect, I am not convinced by the editors' view that the men named in connection with poultry in sheets A-B-C were necessarily *bringing* chickens or geese to the *praetorium*. It seems to me more probable – and perfectly possible so to restore the text – that the soldiers were purchasing poultry *from* the prefect.

14 It is generally assumed that the word *missio*, 'discharge', was applied in the Roman army only to the discharge of a soldier as a veteran, whereas the end of an officer's service would be referred to just as 'receiving a successor', cf. Devijver 1992: 212ff. Thus too Bowman & Thomas 1996: 320f., who restore the name of the person discharged as *Flavi[ni]*, a name that occurs again in this document, line 92: 'we have no indication of his rank but the fact that he was discharged suggests someone below equestrian officer rank'. However, Sallust (*B. Jug.* 64.1) uses the term for C. Marius, legate in Numidia, requesting his *missio* from the proconsul Metellus; and Suetonius (*D. Iul.* 7.1) for Julius Caesar, as quaestor in Further Spain, requesting his *missio* from the governor. Further, two passages in the legal codes, *CJ* 10.53(52).11. pr. and *CTh* 8.5.23.pr., apply the term to the retirement of *archiatri* and persons serving in *officia palatina* respectively. Hence there is no obstacle to restoring the name of an equestrian officer here. Genialis is the only other Flavius known to have served at Vindolanda.

15 On the translation cf. Adams 1995: 121f. The difficulty he finds with 'the image of an equestrian officer in hiding in the undergrowth', as the letter is interpreted in *TV* II, might of course be less serious if the writer were the freedman Gentilis, as suggested above.

16 On the Roman Matronalia: *RE* 14.2 (1930) cols. 2306-9. For the Matronae in the Rhineland, cf. Saddington 1999: 158ff., with copious references. Cf. also below, *Religion*.

17 I owe to Paul Holder this way to interpret the fragmentary text: *decurion[ibus . . .] i· cerv[esae . . .]*.

18 This is shown by the *Feriale Duranum* (where the festival is called *rosaliae signorum*).

19 Kajanto 1965: 227; Lörincz 1999: 144f.

20 L. Publilius Celsus (*PIR2* P 1049) was highly esteemed by Trajan, who honoured him with a statue at Rome, along with other men who held major military commands (Dio 68.16.2), but nothing is known of his career apart from his consulships, the first in 102, the second in 113. Syme 1988: 491n. suggested that he might have been governor of Britain. A man called Celsus crops up twice in the writing-tablets, once as having been visited by Brocchus (1453) and once as the addressee of a draft letter by Priscinus, prefect of the First Tungrians (1332). But there is a simpler identification, see below.

21 Rivet & Smith 1979:185ff.; 208; 268 (where the name is emended to 'Bibra' and the site identified with the fort of Beckfoot on the Solway Firth). On Kirkbride: Bellhouse 1963; Birley, E. & Bellhouse 1975; Jones, G.D.B. 1982: 283f.; Higham & Jones 1985: 26f., 29; Jones, G.D.B. 1989; 1991: 102. On the meaning of 'Briga': Rivet & Smith 1979: 278.

22 Rivet & Smith 1979: 420f.
23 Cf. n. 20, above.
24 *ILS* 2001=*CIL* XVI 48=*RIB* II 2401.1.
25 Pliny, *Letters* 3.8; Birley, A.R. 2001B: 26.
26 Wild 1993: 76ff.
27 Driel-Murray 1993: 32ff., 43ff.
28 Wild 1993: 84.
29 Here it must be confessed that my doubts about the reading *filiolus* in Severa's birthday invitation, 292 (Birley, A.R. 1991: 101), firmly dismissed by the editors, were indeed unfounded: the same word is used by Brocchus in 1329.
30 Wild 1993: 83.
31 For the reading 'by your descendants', *per [pos]teritatem* see Tomlin 1996: 462.
32 *CIL* III 4360, Arrabona: he was prefect of an *ala* there, cf. Epilogue.
33 *RE* 2A.1 (1921) cols. 1108-9.
34 Arrian, *Cyneg.* 3ff. (my own translation); cf. on *vertragi RE* 8A.2 (1958) cols. 1662-8.
35 Cf. Seaward 1993: 112; Pearce forthcoming.
36 Coulston & Phillips 1988: nos. 6, 303; Patricia Birley in Birley, A. & Blake 2000: 30 & fig. 31, cf. 16.
37 For the vessels see esp. Hilgers 1969, with exhaustive quotation of all ancient sources. He does not include *ovaria*, not surprisingly, since, as the editors of *TV* II note, its only Latin attestation referred to *ova* in a non-literal sense, in the circus; they also cite a papyrus where the Greek form seems to mean egg-cup. In *TV* II 194 it could just as well mean a large container, e.g. for pickling eggs. As Hilgers shows, almost all these words tended to have variable meanings (e.g. *acetabulum* was not just for vinegar).
38 Cf. above, n. 20, 24.
39 Empel and Magusanus: Roymans & Derks 1993; Roymans 1996: 90ff.; on Magusanus cf. also valuable remarks by Saddington 1999: 164f.
40 Phillips & Coulston 1988: 14, nos. 32-3.
41 Adams 1995: 129.
42 Cf. Pliny, *Letters* 7.22, recommending Cornelius Minicianus to Pompeius Falco, later governor of Britain, then governing Judaea, for a military tribunate. He calls his protégé 'an ornament of my region, both by reason of his rank and of his character' and stresses that 'he loves (liberal) studies', *amat studia*. It will also be recalled that Pliny arranged a tribunate for Suetonius from Neratius Marcellus, which Suetonius then declined to take up, *Letters* 3.8.

8 Epilogue

1 Strobel 1987: 272ff.
2 *CIL* III 4360; Birley, A.R. 1997B: 50ff.
3 Roxan 1995.
4 Breeze & Dobson 2000: 88ff., 117ff.
5 Cf. the summary in *VRR* IV.1, 6.
6 Birley, R. *et al.* 1998: 12ff.; Blake 2001: 7ff.
7 Holder 1982: 117.
8 Birley, A.R. 1981: 168ff.
9 Birley, A.R. 1979: 107f., 110; *RE* 9A.1 (1961) 408-415. The Vindolanda examples are *RIB* 1697-9 and Birley, R. 1993: 74, nos. 2 & 3. Ross 1967: 372ff. and Birley, E. 1986: 62ff. prefer a native British origin for this deity.

Abbreviations and bibliography

AA4,5   *Archaeologia Aeliana*, 4th, 5th series

Adams, J.N. 1995 'The language of the Vindolanda Tablets: an interim report', *JRS* 85: 86-134

Adams, J.N. 1996 'The interpretation of *souxtum* at *Tab. Vindol.* II 301.3', *ZPE* 110: 238

Alföldy, G. 1968 *Die Hilfstruppen der römischen Provinz Germania Inferior* (Düsseldorf: Rheinland-Verlag)

BAR British Archaeological Reports

Bellhouse, R.L. 1975 'The Roman site at Kirkbride, Cumbria', *CW2* 75: 58-90

Bidwell, P. 1985 *The Roman Fort of Vindolanda* (London: HBMC England)

Bidwell, P. 1997 *Roman Forts in Britain* (London: Batsford)

Bidwell, P. 1999 'A summary of recent research on Hadrian's Wall', in Bidwell, P., ed., 1999: 7-36

Bidwell, P., ed. 1999 *Hadrian's Wall 1989-1999. A Summary of Recent Excavations and Research prepared for The Twelfth Pilgrimage of Hadrian's Wall, 14-21 August 1999* (Carlisle: CWAAS & SAN)

Birley, A(ndrew) 1997 *Security: Locks and Keys. VRR* IV.2 (Greenhead: RAM Pub)

Birley, A. 2001 *Vindolanda's Military Bath Houses. Report on the pre-Hadrianic military bath house found in 2000, with analysis of the early third-century bath house excavated in 1970/71, and possible sites of other bath houses* (Greenhead: RAM Pub)

Birley, A. & Blake, J. 2000 *Vindolanda. The Excavations of 1999. Interim Report on the work on the Southern Defences of Stone Fort Two* (Bardon Mill: Vindolanda Trust)

Birley, A(nthony) R. 1979 *The People of Roman Britain* (London: Batsford)

Birley, A.R. 1981 *The Fasti of Roman Britain* (Oxford: Clarendon Press)

Birley, A.R. 1990A 'Vindolanda: Neue Ausgrabungen 1985-1986', in H. Vetters & M. Kandler, ed., *Akten des 14. Limeskongresses Carnuntum 1986* (Vienna: Österreichische Akademie der Wissenschaften): 333-40

Birley, A.R. 1990B *Officers of the Second Augustan Legion in Britain* (Cardiff: National Museum of Wales)

Birley, A.R. 1991A 'Vindolanda: new writing tablets', in Maxfield & Dobson, eds.: 16-20

Birley, A.R. 1991B 'Vindolanda: notes on some new writing tablets', *ZPE* 88: 87-102

Birley, A.R. 1993 'A review of the tablets, by Periods', in *VRR* II: 18-72

Birley A.R. 1997A 'Supplying the Batavians at Vindolanda', in Groenman-van Wateringe, W. *et al.*, eds., *Roman Frontier Studies 1995: Proceedings of the XVIth International Congress of Roman Frontier* (Oxford: Oxbow Monograph 91): 273-280

Birley, A.R. 1997B *Hadrian. The Restless Emperor* (London & New York: Routledge)

Birley, A.R. 1998 'A new tombstone from Vindolanda', *Britannia* 29: 299-306

Birley, A.R. 1999 'The Vindolanda writing tablets', in Bidwell, P., 1999: 37-47

Birley, A.R. 2001A 'The names of the Batavians and Tungrians in the *Tabulae Vindolandenses*', in Grünewald, T., ed.: 241–260

Birley, A.R. 2001B 'A band of brothers: equestrian officers in the Vindolanda tablets', *Electrum* (Crácow) 5: 11–30

Birley, A.R. 2001C 'The Anavionenses', in Higham, N.J., ed. 2001: 15-24

Birley, E. 1953 *Roman Britain and the Roman Army. Collected papers* (Kendal: Titus Wilson)

Birley, E. 1961 *Research on Hadrian's Wall* (Kendal: Titus Wilson)

Birley, E. 1963 'The Thorngrafton hoard', *Numismatic Chronicle*, 7th ser., 3: 61-6

Birley, E. 1986 'The deities of Roman Britain', in Temporini, H. & Haase, W., eds., *Aufstieg und Niedergang der römischen Welt* II. 18.1 (Berlin & New York: de Gruyter): 3-112

Birley, E. 1988 *The Roman Army: Papers 1929-1986* (Amsterdam: Gieben)

Birley, E. 1993 'The auxiliaries', in *VRR* II: 4-9

Birley, E. & Bellhouse, R.L. 1963 'The Roman site at Kirkbride, Cumberland', *CW*2 63: 126-139

Birley, R. 1962 'Some excavations at Chesterholm-Vindolanda', *AA4* 40: 97-103

Birley, R. 1970 'Excavations at Chesterholm-Vindolanda 1967-1969', *AA4* 48: 97-155

Birley, R. 1973 'Vindolanda-Chesterholm 1969-1972: some important material from the vicus', *AA5* 1: 111-22

Birley, R. 1977 *Vindolanda: A Roman Frontier Post on Hadrian's Wall* (London: Thames & Hudson)

Birley, R. 1993 'Inscriptions, brands, graffiti', in *VRR* II: 73-102

Birley, R. 1994 *The Early Wooden Forts: excavations of 1973-1976 and 1985-1989, with some additional details from the excavations of 1991-1993. VRR* I

Birley, R. 1995 *The Making of Modern Vindolanda with The Life and Work of Anthony Hedley 1777-1835* (Greenhead: RAM Pub)

Birley, R. 1996 *The Weapons. VRR* IV.1

Birley, R. 1998 *The Fort at the Rock. Magna and Carvoran on Hadrian's Wall* (Greenhead: RAM Pub)

Birley, R. 1999A *Roman Records from Vindolanda on Hadrian's Wall* (3rd ed., Greenhead: RAM Pub)

Birley, R. 1999B *Writing Materials. VRR* IV.4

Birley, R. 2000 *Chesterholm. From a clergyman's cottage to Vindolanda's Museum 1830-2000* (Greenhead: RAM Pub)

Birley, R., Birley, Andrew & Blake, J. 1999 *The 1998 Excavations at Vindolanda. The Praetorium Site. Interim Report* (Greenhead: RAM Pub)

Birley, R. & Birley, A. 1994 'Four new writing tablets from Vindolanda', *ZPE* 100: 431-446

Birley, R., Blake, J. & Birley, Andrew 1998 *The 1997 Excavations at Vindolanda. The Praetorium Site. Interim Report* (Greenhead: RAM Pub)

Blake, J. 1999 *The Tools. VRR* IV.3

Blake, J. 2001 *The Southern Defences of Stone Fort Two, with the Circular Huts and Other Features* (Greenhead: RAM Pub)

Bowman, A.K. 1994 *Life and Letters on the Roman Frontier: Vindolanda and its People* (London: British Museum Press)

Bowman, A.K. & Thomas, J.D. 1983 *Vindolanda: The Latin Writing tablets* (London: Society for the Promotion of Roman Studies); with contributions by Adams, J.N. and Tapper, R.; also abbreviated *TV* I

Bowman, A.K. & Thomas, J.D. 1994 *The Vindolanda Writing Tablets (Tabulae Vindolandenses* II) (London: British Museum Press); with contributions by Adams, J.N.; also abbreviated *TV* II

Bowman, A.K. & Thomas, J.D. 1996 'New writing tablets from Vindolanda', *Britannia* 27: 299-328

Bowman, A.K., Thomas, J.D. & Wright, R.P. 'The Vindolanda writing-tablets', *Britannia* 5: 471-80

Breeze, D.J., 1974 'The organisation of the career structure of the *immunes* and *principales* of the Roman army', *Bonner Jahrbücher* 174: 245-92

Breeze, D.J. & Dobson, B. 2000 *Hadrian's Wall* (4th ed., London: Penguin)

Brewer, R.J. ed. 2000 *Roman Fortresses and their Legions* (Cardiff: National Museums & Galleries of Wales)

Caruana, I. 1997 'Maryport and the Flavian conquest of north Britain', in Wilson, R.J.A., ed., *Roman Maryport and its Setting. Essays in Memory of Michael G. Jarrett* (Maryport: CWAAS, extra series, 28): 40-51

CIL Corpus Inscriptionum Latinarum (Berlin: Akademie der Wissenschaften, 1863ff.)

Clarke, J. 1958 'Roman and Native, A.D. 80-122', in Richmond, I.A., ed.: 28-59

Coulston, J.C. & Phillips, E.J. 1988 *Corpus Signorum Imperii Romani. Great Britain*. I, fasc. 6. *Hadrian's Wall West of the North Tyne, and Carlisle* (Oxford: Oxford University Press)

CWAAS: Cumberland & Westmorland Antiquarian and Archaeological Society *CW2 Transactions of the Cumberland & Westmorland Antiquarian & Archaeological Society*, 2nd series

Daniels, C.M., ed. 1989 *The Eleventh Pilgrimage of Hadrian's Wall 26 August-1 September 1989* (Newcastle upon Tyne: SAN & CWAAS)

Devijver, H. 1976-1993 *Prosopographia Militiarum Equestrium, vols. I-V* (Leuven: Universitaire Pers)

Devijver, H. 1992 *The Equestrian Officers of the Roman Army*, (vol. II) (Stuttgart: Steiner)

Driel-Murray, C. van, *et al.* 1993 *Preliminary Reports on the Leather, Textiles, Environmental Evidence and Dendrochronology. VRR* III

Driel-Murray, C. van 1993 'The Leatherwork', in Driel-Murray *et al.*, 1993: 1-75

Eck, W. 1999 'The Bar-Kokhba revolt: the Roman point of view', *JRS* 89: 76-89

Funari, P.P.A. 1991 'Dressel 20 amphora inscriptions found at Vindolanda: the reading of the unpublished evidence', in Maxfield & Dobson: 65-72

Grünewald, T., ed. 2001 *Germania Inferior. Besiedlung, Gesellschaft und Wirtschaft an der Grenze der römisch-germanischen Welt* (Berlin-New York: W. de Gruyter)

Grünewald, T., forthcoming 'Gallia Belgica oder Germania Inferior? Zur Frage nach der Zugehörigkeit der Tungri'

HA Historia Augusta

Hassall, M.W.C. 1970 'Batavians and the Roman conquest of Britain', *Britannia* 1: 131-6

Hassall, M.W.C. 2000 'Pre-Hadrianic legionary dispositions in Britain', in Brewer, R.J., ed.: 51-67

Higgs, W. 2001 'Catalogue of animal-imprinted ceramic building-materials', in Birley, Andrew 2001: 51-64

Higham, N.J., ed. 2001 *Archaeology of the Roman Empire. A tribute to the life and works of Professor Barri Jones* (Oxford: BAR International Series 940)

Higham, N.J. & Jones, B. 1985 *The Carvetii* (Gloucester: Sutton)

Hilgers, W. 1969 *Lateinische Gefässnamen. Bezeichnungen, Funktion und Form römischer Gefässe nach den antiken Schriftquellen* (Düsseldorf: Rheinland-Verlag)

Hodgson, G.W.I. 1976 *The Animals of Vindolanda* (Haltwhistle: Barcombe Publications)

Hodgson, G.W.I. 1977 *Vindolanda: The Animal Remains 1970-1975* (Bardon Mill: Barcombe Publications)

Holder, P.A., 1980 *Studies in the Auxilia of the Roman Army from Augustus to Trajan* (Oxford: BAR International Series 70)

Holder, P.A., 1982 *The Roman Army in Britain* (London: Batsford)

ILS H. Dessau, *Inscriptiones Latinae Selectae* (Berlin: Weidmann, 1892-1916)

Jackson, K.H. 1982 'Brigomaglos and St. Briog', *AA5* 10: 61-5

Jones, B.W. 1992 *The Emperor Domitian* (London: Routledge)

Jones, G.D.B. 1982 'The Solway frontier: interim report 1976-1981', *Britannia* 13: 283-97

Jones, G.D.B. 1989 'The western Stanegate', in Daniels, ed.: 92-5

Jones, G.D.B. 1991 'The emergence of the Tyne-Solway frontier', in Maxfield & Dobson, edd.: 98-107

JRS Journal of Roman Studies (London)

Kajanto, I. 1965 *The Latin Cognomina* (Helsinki: Societas Scientiarum Fennica)

Keppie, L.J.F. 2000A 'Legio VIIII in Britain: the beginning and the end', in Brewer, R.J. ed.: 83-100

Keppie, L.J.F. 2000B 'Legiones II Augusta, VI Victrix, IX Hispana, XX Valeria Victrix', in Le Bohec, Y. ed.: 25-37

Le Bohec, Y. ed. 2000 *Les légions de Rome sous le Haut-Empire*, 2 vols. (Lyon & Paris: De Boccard)

Locher, A. & Rottländer, R.C.A. 1985 'Überlegungen zur Entstehungsgeschichte der *Naturalis Historia* des älteren Plinius und die Schrifttäfelchen von Vindolanda', *Lebendige Alertumswissenschaft. Festgabe . . . H. Vetters* (Vienna: Adolf Holzhausens Nfg.): 140-7

Lörincz, B. 1999 *Onomasticon Provinciarum Europae Latinarum*, II: *Cabalicius-Ixius* (Vienna: Forschungsgesellschaft Wiener Stadtarchäologie)

Lörincz, B. 2000 *Onomasticon Provinciarum Europae Latinarum*, III: *Labareus-Pythea* (Vienna: Forschungsgesellschaft Wiener Stadtarchäologie)

Lörincz, B. & Redö, F. 1994 *Onomasticon Provinciarum Europae Latinarum*, I: *Aba-Bysanus* (Budapest: Archaeolingua Alapítvány)

Maxfield, V.A. & Dobson, M.J. 1991 *Roman Frontier Studies 1989: Proceedings of the XVth International Congress of Roman Frontier Studies* (Exeter: University of Exeter Press)

Mócsy, A. 1983 *Nomenclator Provinciarum Europae Latinarum et Galliae Cisalpinae cum indice inverso* (Budapest: Dissertationes Pannonicae III.1)

Neumann, G. 1976 'Bataver', *Reallexikon der Germanischen Altertumskunde* (2nd ed., Berlin: de Gruyter) II: 91

Oliver, J.H. 1989 *Greek Constitutions of Early Roman Emperors from Inscriptions and Papyri* (Philadelphia: American Philosophical Society)

Pearce, J. forthcoming 'Food as substance and symbol in the Roman army: a case study from Vindolanda', in P. Freeman, ed., *Roman Frontier Studies 2000. Proceedings of the 18th International Congress of Roman Frontier Studies, Amman 2000* (Oxford: BAR Int. Series)

PIR2 E. Groag, A. Stein, L. Petersen *et al.*, eds., *Prosopographia Imperii Romani* (Berlin: de Gruyter, 2nd ed., 1933ff.)

Raepsaet-Charlier, M.-Th., 1991 'Cn. Iulius Agricola: Mise au point proso-pographique', in H. Temporini & W. Haase, edd., *Aufstieg und Niedergang der römischen Welt* II.33.3 (Berlin & New York: de Gruyter): 1807-57

RAMPub Roman Army Museum Publications

RE Paulys *Realencyclopädie der classischen Altertumswissenschaft*, edd. G. Wissowa *et al.* (Stuttgart: Metzler, 1892-1980)

RIB I-II R.G. Collingwood & R.P. Wright, eds., *The Roman Inscriptions of Britain*, I, *Inscriptions on Stone* (Oxford: Clarendon Press, 1965); 2nd ed. R.S.O. Tomlin (Stroud: Sutton, 1995); S.S. Frere *et al.* eds., II, *Instrumentum Domesticum* (Gloucester & Stroud: Sutton, 1990-5)

Richmond, I.A., ed. 1958 *Roman and Native in North Britain* (Edinburgh: Nelson)

Rivet, A.L.F. & Smith, *c.*1979 *The Place-Names of Roman Britain* (London: Batsford)

Ross, A. 1967 *Pagan Celtic Britain* (London: Routledge & Kegan Paul)

Roxan, M.M. 1985 'The Roman military diploma', in Bidwell, P. 1985: 93-102

Roymans, N.1996 'The sword or the plough. Regional dynamics in the romanisa-tion of Belgic Gaul and the Rhineland area', in Roymans, N., ed., *From the Sword to the Plough. Three studies on the earliest Romanisation of Northern Gaul* (Amsterdam: Amsterdam University Press): 9-126

Roymans N. 2001 'The Lower Rhine *triquetrum* coinage and the ethnogenesis of the Batavi', in Grünewald, T. 2001: 93-145

Roymans, N. & Derks, T. 1993 'Der Tempel von Empel: Ein-Hercules-Heiligtum im Batavergebiet', *Archaologisches Korrespondenzblatt* 23: 479-92

SAN Society of Antiquaries of Newcastle upon Tyne

Schulze, W. 1933: *Zur Geschichte lateinischer Eigennamen* (2nd ed., Berlin: Weidmann)

Seaward, M. 1993: 'The Environmental material', in *VRR* III: 91-119

Shotter, D.C.A. 2000: 'Petillius Cerialis in northern Britain', *Northern History* 36: 189-98

Speidel, M.A. 1992 'Roman army pay scales', *JRS* 82: 87-106

Speidel, M..A. 1995 'Ferox: legionary commander or governor? A note on Tab. Vindol. II 154', in R. Frei-Stolba & M.A. Speidel, edd., *Römische Inschriften – Neufunde, Neulesungen und Neuinterpretationen: Festschrift fur Hans Lieb* (Basel & Berlin: Reinhardt): 43-54

Speidel, M.A. 1996 *Die römischen Schreibtafeln von Vindonissa* (Brugg: Gesellschaft Pro Vindonissa)

Speidel, M.P. 1987 *Guards of the Roman Armies. An essay on the singulares of the provinces* (Bonn: Habelt)

Speidel, M.P. 1992 *Roman Army Studies 2* (Stuttgart: Steiner)

Speidel, M.P. 1994 *Riding for Caesar. The Roman emperors' horse guard* (London: Batsford)

Speidel, M.P. 1998 'The Risingham *praetensio*', *Britannia* 29: 356-9

Strobel, K., 1987 'Anmerkungen zur Geschichte der Bataverkohorten in der hohen Kaiserzeit', *ZPE* 70: 271-292

Syme, R. 1958 *Tacitus* (Oxford: Clarendon Press)

Syme, R. 1988 *Roman Papers* IV-V (Oxford: Clarendon Press)

Tomlin, R.S.O. 1996 'The Vindolanda tablets', *Britannia* 27: 459-63

Tomlin, R.S.O. 1998 'Roman manuscripts from Carlisle: the ink-written tablets', *Britannia* 29: 31-84

TV I, II see Bowman & Thomas 1983, 1994, above

VRR: *Vindolanda Research Reports*, new series, I-III. *The Early Wooden Forts* (Bardon Mill: RAMPub); IV (in fascicules). *The Small Finds* (Greenhead: RAM Pub); so far published:

VRR I Birley, R. 1994 *The Early Wooden Forts: the excavations of 1973-1976 and 1985-1989, with some additional details from the excavations of 1991-1993*

VRR II Birley, E., Birley, R. & Birley, A. 1993 *Reports on the Auxiliaries, Inscriptions, Brands and Graffiti*

VRR III Driel-Murray, C. van, *et al.* 1993 *Preliminary Reports on the Leather, Textiles, Environmental Evidence and Dendrochronology*

VRR IV.1 Birley, R. 1996 *The Weapons*

VRR IV.2 Birley, Andrew 1997 *Security: the Keys and Locks*

VRR IV.3 Blake, J. 1999 *The Tools*

VRR IV.4 Birley, R. 1999B *The Writing Materials*

Wild, J.P., 1993 'The Textiles', in *VRR* III: 76-90

Willems, W.J.M. 1986 *Romans and Batavians. A Regional Study in the Dutch East River Area* (originally published as a long article in two parts, 1981 and 1984; 2nd ed., Dissertation, Amsterdam University)

ZPE: *Zeitschrift für Papyrologie und Epigraphik* (Cologne)

Index

Items in the Preface and persons later than the nineteenth century are not included. Roman citizens with more than one name are listed under their *nomen*, e.g. Flavius. The following abbreviations are used:

Bat. Batavian(s); cent. centurion; corr. correspondent; dec. decurion; eq. off. equestrian officer; gov. governor; i.c. in charge of; *opt. optio*; pref. prefect; qu. quoted.

1 Personal names

2 Geographical Names

(some names on page 39 and in the maps are omitted)

3 General

Addendum

New writing tablets found in 2001 include:

Inv. 01-15: another (fragmentary) strength report, from one of the outer Period I ditches, clearly also of coh. I Tungrorum, under the same prefect, [Julius Ver]ecundus, with 6 centurions.

Inv. 01-39: an account, from a Period IV level, evidently in the *praetorium* of the second fort of the Tungrians. It names among others the *vexillarius* Tagomas, whose name is also so spelled (rather than Tagamas as in *TV* II 181) on an amphora handle found nearby, and Victor *venator*, 'the huntsman'.